Tracy

Brian Dawtrey

With best wishes

B. Dawtrey

amazon

New Generation Publishing

About Brian Dawtrey

Born 1928. Married Jo in 1948.

After military service 12 years family farming in England.

24 years working in Overseas Aid in Africa, initiating food production schemes.

Implementing soil, water and wildlife conservation.

16 years Honorary Wildlife Ranger.

A past Chairman of the Wildlife Conservation Society of Zambia.

Wife Cicely May (Jo) Dawtrey

Born 1929. Produced a nuclear family of 16.

Farmer, teacher, Education Officer of the WLCSZ.

An initiator of the Chongololo programme of wildlife education for African primary schools.

CHAPTER ONE

1967

Jo and I had become soul-mates during WWII. We were of that post-war young generation that had survived the Nazi onslaught and deprivation, and had an ambition 'to build a new world'. We were of a new generation; **Born Free;** free of the aristocracy, free of parental domination with their religious fervour, free health services, free education [baring a few Public Schools], and free of stuffy old pre-war society. Jo as a nineteen year old said "Brian, what I'd love to do is to live in a Gypsy caravan and just **disappear**; with you". Well; now I think about it I had always aspired as a small child, to explore the world about me; get on a steam train and just go; anywhere. At age nineteen we got married. We took an oath in church, to support each other, through thick and thin, which was a serious undertaking in those post-war days. And so we eventually ended up in Zambia, after six years in Tanzania, on a British Government Overseas Aid Scheme. We did have a caravan in Zambia, but we did not manage to **disappear**! We were 'posted' to Luanshya on the Copperbelt, not to mine copper but to organise schemes for growing food in the surrounding rural district. There was trouble between the Prime Minister Iain Smith of Southern Rhodesia and the British Government, and the border with Zambia was closed. Unfortunately Rhodesia was Zambia's primary food supply of maize the staple diet of Africans. Brian was a graduate in agriculture and an ex farm manager in Norfolk, 'the man for the job'.

The next eleven years turned out to be a heck-of-a-life. We found ourselves in a highly industrialised region, heavily populated by expatriates, mainly British mine workers, supported by British-run services. The commercial sector of the economy was extensive and international. However two thirds of the Copperbelt Province was rural, which was my domain, running to a bit more than the size of Wales and sparsely populated by traditional tribal Africans. I was paid on a Zambian Government salary scale with a small supplement paid into my bank account in England by the long suffering UK taxpayer, to encourage us to stick with it. We also enjoyed airfares for our three children's school holidays. So we were not in Zambia for the money, just the experience? I had recently received three months' training in London by the Ministry of Overseas Development, in aerial photo interpretation, and map making by the Department of Overseas Surveys, a wonderfully efficient and beneficial organisation serving the Commonwealth.

Upon our post-independence arrival we found an air of optimism amongst the Zambian Africans, emerging as they were from an era of racial discrimination and victimisation. This had emanated in essence,

1

from within the much hated Federation of Rhodesia and Nyasaland (now Malawi) governed by Sir Roy Welensky. As a result of this exclusion of black people from the development process, the general mass of Zambians were seriously lacking the skills and enterprise such as were commonplace in East Africa, from whence we had come. .

Jo and I were thirty nine years old and already our eighteen year old daughter Caroline was requesting engagement to a shipping agent in Tanga, Tanzania, where she spent her formative years after schooling at St Michael's and St George's School in Iringa. His name was Iain Aitchison, whom we knew very well. However, we had our reservations with such a young girl being under the influence of an older man, but she wanted to live in paradise Tanga with its palm-fringed coral beaches and the sailing club. She also wanted to **disappear**, from UK, like her Mum.

Our son, Richard, at age sixteen and his thirteen year old brother Philip were now sadly, at boarding school in England, following several years at Arusha School in Tanzania. Philip had inherited the thrill of the wild in Tanzania and had become an adventurer, a risk-taker, and a good shot with my .22 calibre rifle, which I had carried on the plane with no questions asked!

Zambia was a modern world as compared to Tanzania and we had a house phone instead of the proverbial 'runner with a fork stick'. It rang,

"Brian, you are called by that Israeli guy – Ben Ami, wants to discuss your plan for their co-operative."

"OK. I am not planning their co-operative just supporting it. They want roads, a small dam for their poultry and pigs' water supply and some bush clearing to facilitate tractor ploughing. Above all they hate pigs and they want me to design a pig unit."

"So somebody must have told them you used to be a pig farmer then?"

"Yes. They have no idea about pig husbandry but there is a big market for pork in the Copperbelt cities. I will design them a cheap pig house. Good climate for pigs!"

"Brian, looks like you've been recruited to help the Jews again. Correct me if I'm wrong, but weren't you sent to Palestine with the Royal Warwickshire Regiment at the end of the war to protect the Jews, whilst they took the farm-land off the Palestinian Arabs?"

"That's right. It was 1947 we were there but it turned out that we had to protect ourselves instead from the Jews. They must have picked up bad habits from their incarceration by the Nazis. A gang of Jewish terrorists declared war on US, Menachem Begin it was, a guerrilla leader. Some of my trainees were killed by the Jews, as well as two of our sergeants who were publically hanged in the town square. Then in 1948 the State of Israel was declared by the U.N. with the condition that they set aside land for the Palestinian refugees."

"Hope you have better luck with your pig units!"

"I've met the Israeli team and their families living here in Luanshya and they are a happy, friendly crowd. They have invited us to visit them in Israel when we go on leave in three years time. The trouble is that they don't like being told anything. Ben Ami told me that they wanted to trial cotton growing as a cash crop. I told him that Mufulira Agricultural Research Station have already done trials on cotton and found that we were too far south and at too high an altitude. They are going ahead anyway."

"So you've got two bulldozers? Wow! Where did you get them from?"

"It's a surprise to me too Jo. It's my technical boss in Lusaka, Norman Beaumont. He has enlisted me into his Department of Rural Development as a Land Planning Officer, not in the Department of Agricultural like the others round here. So I am not an Advisor but a Doer!"

"I can heartily confirm that! You are also a dreamer. Your school friend John Ashford told me that your nickname at school was Dreamy. How astute high school kids are, they were right. That's why you are a good Planning Officer. Your Dad was a dreamer too, designed and made the most gorgeous caravans, everyone wants one still. They were very expensive, the Rolls Royce of caravans, weren't they."

"My Director sent me two Caterpillar D7 bulldozers plus a foreman, Thomas. I have been advised that I am to commence building dams on Mufulira State Ranch, a vast 23,000 acre site of open *Brachystegia* woodland, much of it cleared and used for making charcoal for the copper mine smelters."

"What do you know about building dams, for goodness sake?"

"They've sent me a Rhodesian brochure on how to build earth dams. I've got a steep learning curve ahead. I have also been advised that a land clearing project is required near Luanshya for creating a dairy farm to supply fresh milk for the town. I was told to make a plan, catering for an enlisted Italian manager to operate a modern milking parlour. All this responsibility on a miserable O.S.A.S., salary of £2,085 per annum! OK and a free house."

About that free house; modern, with an extensive garden, in the suburbs of the Roan Antelope Mine township of Luanshya. Luanshya town is a European style shopping and services centre lined with fabulous Jacaranda trees of intense purple blossom, a truly beautiful town, and with a mosquito free environment. There were good schools, previously 100% 'white' but now destined to slowly change colour as African education takes priority.

Our house had been previously occupied by a white family of a somewhat "lower-order" it was said, and was infested by bed bugs, not to mention baboon spiders, renowned for their size, hairy bodies and padded feet, one of which was quite a lump in our bed one night, because of its golf-ball size! We were advised that they were "quite harmless".

3

Since our boxes had not arrived from Tanga Tanzania, where we left two months ago, we were camping out, in a sense, but we gradually resolved the bed bug discomfort more by accident than insecticide. We had joined the library of the Womens Service League and obtained a somewhat over-thumbed explorer book about Australia. It seemed Australian explorers had an even tougher time than the African version. This book had suffered from time and use, such that the pages were spongy and odorous. The offending bed bugs however, adored the comfy blanket experience and we had a harvest each morning from the bedside table, such that the population eventually died out. Fortunately for us our gigantic, hairy, baboon spider had been more sophisticated in its overnight comfort requirements. Since I had now been gazetted as an Hon. Wildlife Ranger, following such appointment in Tanzania, I was morally obliged to refrain from crushing the spider with my mallet.

We decided we had better go and have a look at the mine to see what the fuss was all about. Roan Antelope Mine was a monster in the African countryside. It employed thousands of both Africans and British workers. Nearby was a dam called Makoma Dam which was converted into the Sailing Club, which filled us with optimism as ex. tropical ocean sailors.

Just before I was born, a 'white hunter' passed by, shot a Roan Antelope which fell on some rock that shone with 'fool's gold'. One thing led to another and more copper as well as malachite was found at Bwana Makubwa near Ndola. Such a mineral rich area attracted investors first in Ndola, then in Luanshya 20 miles to the south. This Luanshya mine was named Roan Antelope Mine. Then we visited the cemetery; thick as thieves they lay there, in hundreds and hundreds with their suitcases, tools and helmets on top of each man's mound as a last reminder, or to help him find a job on the other side.

In the evening, we met up with Roy Noble, passing through from Tanzania. He knew everyone in Mbeya where we used to live. He loaned us a fridge from the hostel in Ndola and a book to pass the time awaiting our boxes to arrive, *"Kenya's Warning"* by Christopher Wilson (1954). It was a very good prophecy of grim events to come, namely the Mau- Mau Rebellion.

We decided to go out to our current survey area called Kafulafuta where we were opening up the area for the Israeli Co-operative Farming Scheme, a kind of Kibbutzim. My African field- Staff were busy pegging out road alignments, which I had delineated on aerial photographs, for my two bulldozers to clear. Jo was with me, as always, thus arousing some interest amongst the Technical Assistants. They all spoke the national language English, but the labourers did not and I tended to revert to Kiswahili out of habit. However Kiswahili was an unknown language in Zambia, I was no longer *Bwana* but *Mukwai,* not *Jambo* but *Endita Mukwai* = Hello Sir. Everything was a learning curve. The absence of

4

Kiswahili does indicate how historically disconnected Central Africa was from East Africa. There was now a need for me to organise a serious field training course for the junior staff in the basics of simple land surveying. There seemed to be additional survey equipment available in Ndola, such it was, that we were now living in an industrialised nation.

So there we were, Jo and I, two soul-mates dependent upon the goodwill of a new democratic One Party State Government, entrusted to initiate rural development schemes, using government money. How much land was there available? Zambia is at least the size of Europe; however, my piece was about the size of Wales. Surprisingly the population of this vast nation was only 3.5 million in 1967. As to the climate, superb. Communications; roads and railways to the south were very good, providing trade and total dependence upon Rhodesia and South Africa. There was an International Airport in the capital Lusaka linked to Ndola.

12th August 1967

At last letters from our three children in the UK arrived. It had been a month since we left but we were glad that they were not with us to suffer the confusion and uncertainty. They were having a great time on our friends' the Friswells, farm until the autumn school term started at Princethorp College, Rugby. Apparently the boys managed to get an old derelict Ford Prefect car going from the barn and drove it all over the farm. Unfortunately they crashed into a farm electricity pole and "created a lightning display", which shorted the supply to the milking parlour. They were sentenced; to hard labour in the milking parlour. Caroline, now 18, was working as a dental nurse in Coventry and would come to Luanshya soon, at our expense now that she had finished school.

The local political scene was dominated by UNIP; United National Independence Party. A Party Conference in Mulungushi attracted my attention since there were three presidents in attendance; Milton Obote of the Congo where serious trouble was brewing with some 850 refugees in the city of Kitwe, Nyerere of Tanzania and Kenneth Kaunda of Zambia.

Kenneth Kaunda spoke of "Humanism" and spoke the "Common Man" philosophy. He expressed support for Biafra in the Nigerian War, which turned out to be the losing side; the Christian Biafrans were bombed by Muslim Federal B52 bombers. Milton Obote promised a Union of States in the Congo and Julius Nyerere spoke of how he had created peace by abolishing chiefdoms, which didn't go down too well with Kenneth Kaunda.

There were turbulent wars in Africa at the time in Congo, Mozambique (backed by the Chinese), Nigeria, Angola (backed by communist Cuba) and Rhodesia, post U.D.I. Recent wars in Kenya and Uganda and Ethiopia were hopefully 'sorted'. I ventured to classify Zambia also as 'sorted'.

Jo heard a young South African fellow call his driver a "stupid, black bastard," because he had failed to carry his petrol coupons with him. She was horrified of course since we had never heard that kind of parlance before, during our six years living in Tanzania.

<u>22nd August 1967</u>

I spent the day with Jo trekking in Kafulafuta area, checking road alignments for the dozers.

"I need a grader to do this job properly. I will request CWA to supply one."

After much walking we ended up in a village sitting with a family of 4 women, 3 men and 17 children. The language was a problem with these Lamba people. We managed to buy some groundnuts they called *muninga* and some cabbages which they grew in the valley bottom "dambo". We learned that the Lamba lineage was through the female line, hence Chieftainess Ndubeni whom we later met.

29th August 1967

Trekking about in Kafulafuta as usual, checking survey beacons, using the railway to get a bearing, we found strange beacons not seen before which was worrying but could have been Israelis doing their own thing as always. We met up with our dozer supervisor Thomas, for lunch in his Sprite caravan. Thomas was a bearded Australian who lived alone, well not quite alone, but with a liver coloured Pointer dog as a pet, a Duiker and a Bush Baby, the miniature species, with huge dark searching eyes. Thomas referred to Australia as "a land of no background and a lot of purpose". Many people who live alone think up all the conversations they would like to have and there was no stopping Thomas once he got going. He had actually lost the knack of conversation. He had a multitude of literary quotations and condensed good English expressions, giving the impression of intelligence and somewhat inflated self-opinion. Was there ever a wife? Taboo subject; and the only subject that would terminate the onslaught of tales of what he did in Saigon, Jo'burg, Hong Kong, New Zealand, Afghanistan, London and Europe. Having nothing to resemble qualifications or a wife, he had ended up in his 40's with a CWA supplied caravan and two bulldozers. We got soaked in very heavy rain on the way home, which was rare for August. Luanshya's annual rainfall is around 70 inches, a little more than Cornwall, deposited though, in six months.

On the news we heard that a pitched battle had taken place in London at the Chinese Embassy as the Police were attacked by the Chinese with bottles, axes, sticks and bricks. So even swinging Britain felt the pangs of oriental strife. We wondered whether there was any peace anywhere in the world.

All together in Luanshya

The beloved Sally, a Veteran.

Britain was peaceful except for teenager problems with motorbike gangs, skin-heads and the like, now that there was no National Service they were lacking a challenge. We were invited out to supper with twelve colonial service British Agricultural Officers. They were somewhat mystified by our situation. They were all leaving.

1st September 1967

I was trekking the Kafulafuta land-clearing project, as usual, after clearing my office of pointless paperwork I would like to have worked from a caravan like Thomas. Jo would have liked that too, of course. It is curious how the ambition of all educated Africans was to occupy an office chair whilst that of expatriates was to escape from theirs.

Today I found two of my staff drinking *chibuku* in a Bar with our government Land Rover outside. The driver did not partake and laid an official complaint. This was followed later by a complaint by the junior staff about the driver's indiscipline and his age. "He can't stay away from his wife for more than five days." This referred to the fact that the surveyors had to camp out until the job was done. The dozer drivers did a seven day week also. I organised productivity bonuses and they earned really good money doing a 7 day working week.

I took the month's wages out for the thirteen labourers; Kwacha 350 = £175. They told me, in a happy frame of mind that the reason why work had stopped, causing the junior government staff to go in search of a Bar, was that the bulldozers were all at a standstill due to their African Supervisor having been killed in a road accident, caused by a drunk driver. There was a sprinkling of thriving Bars along the main road to the capital, Lusaka. The official statistics of road accidents for the first six months of that year, for a population of 3.5 million was – 175 killed, 1,000 injured 4,690 accidents.

14th September 1967

I spent the day with Jo in a dambo on the new Mufulira Ranch. The 23,000 acre government upper valley ranch lay between the city of Kitwe and the Congo border. I had to locate possible earth dam sites which would be in *dambos*. These are treeless, grassy and pleasant valley bottoms. Having located them on air photos we then searched for them on foot, always with our Sally Spaniel 'at foot'. This involved endless walking through miombo woodland with a compass, and the risk of getting completely lost. On this occasion, a bush fire blew up and swept the area. Fortunately, I left my Land Rover on a bare patch and found it OK. We arrived back, black from soot, after a long trek. Even Sally was exhausted. There seemed to be no wild life left in the woodland but we did find a guinea fowl feather. We also found a glorious raffia palm about 40 ft. high and full of weaver birds feasting on the fruits.

16th September 1967

Dr Hastings Banda, Life President of Malawi, which neighbours Zambia and Rhodesia, spoke on the radio condemning the hypocrisy of Zambians "filling their bellies with beef from South Africa." Banda was despised by all Africans in Zambia for his despotic rule and his talking to leaders in Rhodesia and South Africa. We had South African beef for lunch that day at home, feeling chilly after that very heavy rain storm. I scraped a python skin that I had shot in the garden. We should have eaten the snake to placate Hastings Banda I suppose.

18th September 1967

Letters to Iain Aitchison in Tanga Tanzania, about our boxes produced no response since we left on 12th July. He was jeopardising his chances with our daughter. So we were struggling uncomfortably in our house, hence spending our day in the wilds of Kafulafuta with lunch in Thomas's caravan, with his Bush Baby. This tiny woolly creature with huge globular eyes was like a child's fluffy doll that loves to play its own games and doesn't bite. Thomas, the non-stop talking narcissist bush-whacker enlightened us about life in Tibet, Ceylon and Malaya and recommended that we go to Penang for our next leave for a hot holiday.

Some Africans killed a cow with their axes and carted off the pieces on their bicycles to a feast in the village downstream. Maybe they had taken to Hastings Banda's criticism of Zambians to heart. How different was our life here from anything experienced in the lives of the expatriate mining community nearby!

20th September 1967

I took the Winder family, an agricultural officer of Irish descent, to an intended picnic in the area we had cleared of bush. Unfortunately, they got lost so we had a thankfully quiet afternoon by the Chondwa stream with heavenly birdsong and rumbling thunderstorms in the background. Talking of heaven, the Winders had advised us that their growing young son, an unruly scatter-brain personality, was Jesus re-born and we should not scold him for his ill manners. Long term we would be relieved of this strain due to 'africanisation' of all ex-colonial staff.

21st September 1967

I spent several hours chasing Levi Ngoma, my Kapitao, from village to village in the Kafulafuta area. My Assistant Benson tried to persuade Jo and me to enjoy a pint of *chibuku*, a village alcoholic homemade delight he said, en route to finding Levi Ngoma. I knew about village beer from Tanzania. Benson partook in a 'quickie' and became intoxicated, giving a running discourse on the reputation of some of the Agricultural Officers in the Department, followed by his experiences in Cairo during the War in the army, where he said he met Montgomery. Since he was only in his thirty's this seemed somewhat dubious.

Whilst eating picnic lunch by Chondwe stream at 1.00 pm, Levi turned up on foot from Ichonde the railway station 2 miles away, and advised me that our labourers were off duty today and had gone in search of food, or was it Chibuku (4.5% alcohol), "but they will be back at work at 4.00 am tomorrow morning Sar". He lived in a straw-lined bivouac covered with a groundsheet 10 ft x 8 ft, just outside the Asian shop of Desai in the village.

I told these field supervisors of mine that I was visiting Thomas tomorrow to sign off the bulldozers in favour of a clearing programme for the Kafubu Dairy and then the Forestry Plantations Department. This Kafulafuta work I costed out at Kwacha 4,700 for 47 miles of roadway clearing, Kwacha 100=£50 per mile, very cheap in fact, but with no gravel surfacing. CWA stands for Conex Working Account, this great idea was to create a quasi-government agency with government capital funding and from then on had to finance itself by charging modest rates for work in the public sector i.e. farmers and forestry.

23rd September 1967

The land clearing for the Israeli Scheme was now finished. I found three Agricultural Assistants drunk in the bar in Masaiti, the Ndola Rural District headquarters about 20 miles south of Luanshya in the chief's Native Land area. This rural area constitutes three quarters of the Copperbelt Province and attracts no industrial development because there is no security of tenure. If you invest money in an enterprise in a chief's area, creating employment and a saleable product, you could be out 'on your ear' any day because the Chief had had a heavy night on *chibuku*.

The British colonial government had set up a belt of state owned land through the centre of this vast country called the Line-of-Rail, running from the Copperbelt connecting southwards, to South Africa and westwards to Angola. There was no connection north to East Africa. The isolated vast Northern provinces were undeveloped *miombo* forest; the tsetse fly infested lands of the Bemba people. It was from there that emerged a great leader Kenneth Kaunda. His is a story on its own but basically one of peaceful social development long term.

Resulting from the declaration of U.D.I., United Declaration of Independence, by Iain Smith of Rhodesia, in opposition to the U.K. Government, under Harold Wilson, substantial trade losses occurred between the U.K. and Rhodesia, plus deprivation for Zambia. The figures issued by economists in the U.K. at this time were: Aid to Zambia £13,850.000, £7,000,000 for Air Cargo airlift. Loss of trade with Rhodesia was said to be £23,000,000. Hence the cost to UK taxpayers of U.D.I. was approaching £50,000,000. In 2017 currency, that's about £2 billion pounds according to the *measuringworth* website. Britain was being loyal to its ex-colony.

26th September 1967.

We were now surveying Mufulira Ranch daily for potential dam sites for cattle watering. We, consisted of Jo, Tembo and Masonda my college educated senior staff under training. Tembo was a bit off hand at times with me in the beginning. There was still a general mistrust of 'whites' in this country due to their recent history, something that we did not experience at all in East Africa. It was very hot in the rainy season build-up towards October, the 'suicide month'. 6.00 am to 6.00 pm is daylight hours in the tropics. It was appallingly hot now in the open. I could not survive out on the ranch without my London umbrella and three pints of water. Jo had had her three pints that day but became quite faint by midday. The ranch was 60 miles drive each way from Luanshya.

29th September 1967

President Nyerere of Tanzania was, sadly, reported as urging the nation's youth to "show the way forward" by revolutionary public demonstrations, *a la* Maoism. Jo and I were greatly saddened by news of the nationalising of banks and the sisal industry and Ujamaa, a compulsory rounding up of villagers into communal cropping schemes called Ujamaa Villages.

30th September 1967

The Vice President Simon Kapwepwe visited Kafulafuta area with the Israeli team and Jo and I. He addressed a group of villagers and reporters, finally declaring that Zambians were a nation of drinkers and that the expatriates were golfers. "This is all going to change. We are all going to become a nation of workers. The way to prosperity for Zambia is work, work, and more work." Muttering; *"Wishful thinking!"* Subsequently Jo got him into fits of giggles.

Jo began to question whether we really had any sort of career prospects in this troubled country, not to mention the fact that our children were now away in England, though they would fly out for two school holidays per year whilst still at school. In the outcome, we lived in Zambia for eleven years. I think this was due to our devoted love for each other, facing challenges and with our mutual ambition to create opportunities for 'country folk, which we had been in England. We were also engrossed with our love of 'nature' and the conservation of African wildlife.

I was looking for a parallel to rural Zambia in British history and came across *The Village Labourer,* by D.L.Hammond, 1910. He speaks about the Enclosures 1730-1830, "which converted happy, poor peasants into unhappy destitute labourers". There isn't any sign of this happening in

Africa, yet. We have big companies coming in, as opposed to landed gentry. In Zimbabwe, under Mugabe, we have now seen the 'Landed Gentry' being forcibly evicted and replaced by 'peasantry' with disastrous results. In Saxon times, the land and water was the province of God and the people his tenants with the local chiefs being the 'bailiffs'. This is how it is in the Native Land areas of Zambia. At least today's peasantry have the vote. That changes everything, thanks to the lessons of British history being passed down to its colonies at Independence.

17th October 1967

I started a training course for our junior staff in surveying. We decided, after much anxious debate, to agree to our 18 years old daughter Caroline, going to Scotland with her English boyfriend Geoffrey Friswell, a racing car motorist, whom we knew very well. We were hoping to steer the emotional ship away from her beloved 'Tanga Tanzania days' wedding prospect, our long distance 'shot in the dark'. We failed. I hope today, fifty years on, that Iain will smile at these, my youthful reflections.

Russia landed a spacecraft on Venus. It turns out that the ancient Greeks were misguided in their imaginations, and mine, of beauty and serenity. The Russians advised us that the atmosphere is very dense at 98% carbon dioxide, as indeed Planet Earth used to be before the tropical rain forests grew to clothe the planet from Pole to Pole thus creating oxygen, upon which all animal life today depends for survival. Massive destruction of the remaining rain forests today could threaten our survival, due to low oxygen, no matter what other measures we might take to reduce CO_2 emissions.

24th October 1967

We received a letter from Geoffrey Friswell in England asking for Caroline's hand in marriage. At that time, girls were required to get parental consent under the age of twenty one years.

Today is a National Holiday and great celebrations for Zambia's third year of Independence. The President, affectionately known as K.K. was in Luanshya. "Zambia fought and shed blood for Independence." I gather there was very little. Otherwise his very long speech, after crying into his white handkerchief for the above, became a slander of Vorster of R.S.A. and the Tory Party in the U.K. *I can't just remember why that was; something to do with Britain not re-occupying its colony Rhodesia and evicting Iain Smith I think.* Zambia would police the border with Rhodesia he said, and he "felt sure the Africans down south must envy our democracy here in Zambia."

.

27ᵗʰ October 1967

We received a letter from Iain Aitchison, enclosing one from Caroline requesting her hand in marriage. We were annoyed by this outcome and replied that they must wait until Caroline was twenty one. We had known Iain for longer than Caroline. We were beginning to understand the Asian insistence on arranged marriages being better for long term relationship. Jo wrote a stern letter to Iain following mine. We ended up chatting about Caroline with a young couple over supper. Sandy Mac Lennon and her husband were university educated. Sandy was a teacher and we were a bit shocked when she declared that she didn't have any children of her own because "I don't like children". Apparently it was an academic marriage.

November 1967

The Victorian scramble for Africa seemed to have been re-invented. The Italians were building an oil supply pipeline from Dar es Salaam to the Copperbelt. The West Germans were re-gravelling the Great North Road to Tanzania. The Canadians were training Zambian pilots. The Greeks and Indians were managing Zambian shops and restaurants. British O.S.A.S. Officers were staffing key government departments. The Israelis were managing hotels and settlement schemes. The Chinese were giving floor shows about their Revolution. The British were training the Zambian Army. A Persian engineer, with a British wife lived next door but one. Russians were supplying arms to guerrillas en route to Rhodesia. You might ask what were the Zambians were doing? To which the answer would have to be, **banging the drum**

We celebrated our nineteenth wedding anniversary on the eight, with a splash of South African wine. Everyone was amazed that we had three grown up children 'somewhere' and Jo still looking like a girl of 18 at 38. We went to the Roan Cinema to see *Hercules*!

The Americans landed another Surveyor craft softly on the Moon. It beat me how such a scatter-brained lot managed it. Letters came from home to tell us that my sister Joy had accommodated Iain for 18 days, which must have clinched the deal! Sister Joy said he was hard up and had to put a deposit on the engagement ring before leaving for Nairobi. It seemed more like a game of chess than a whirling romance.

December 1967

Christmas Eve saw us happily united with our three children and our boxes from Tanga. We had a grand party with Peter and Betty Devonald and their friends the Beales. We were all native Brits together for a change, enjoying a candlelight supper followed by party games. The children however, were excited over being 'at home' as they thought of Africa.

Christmas day proved a happy time with not too much self-indulgence but also included a traditional roast turkey and a Christmas cake. Fishing tackle proved the most popular present with the boys. Richard's savings of £5 contributed to his ambition-achieved, a National Record Player. Philip loved his model making. The afternoon was spent with the African boys next door, the Ngenda's, shooting with their bows and arrows, at Philip's model aeroplane.

New Year 1968

For the boys it was all fishing now, in Kafubu and Makoma Dam but there was also some hunting with my .22 rifle. However there was not a lot of game about in the Kafulafuta dambo. Sally Spaniel put up a *kwali* – partridge, and a flock of green pigeons. Philip aged 12 was a better shot than Richard with my rifle but the elder brother was very handy with a catapult and small ball-bearings as well as being much quicker 'off the mark'.

Philip accompanied me camping in the bush on Mufulira Ranch. He loved it and was very reliable. Philip's keenness on adventure and taking risks has turned out to be his life story. Richard did not like taking risks and cared not for futile time-wasting activities but cared more for the welfare of people around him, which has been his life story. As for Caroline, she was a more responsible person and a good organiser and very aware of the welfare of family and people around her. We were all at the Ranch one day when my government Land Rover sank in the wet sand after a storm which meant a thirteen mile walk back in the dusk. Fortunately the others did not join me on the dam site and waited in our car at the ranch house for my return. The Ranch Manager and his wife kept Jo *et al* waiting in our car for four hours; they had a reputation for social reserve. We gathered that they were from the Solwezi Plymouth Brethren Mission which presumably had an ancient connection with the Puritan Protestants of the English civil war and the Mayflower to America.

For the rest of our first Christmas in Zambia, Philip busied himself building models. He became an engineering designer much later. Richard, aged 15 years, got stuck into gardening, getting the home into shape. He continued to do that all his life too and became a hospital manager. Jo provided a strict incentive for this hard labour at nine shillings an hour, plus bonuses for extra effort, in line with Brian's policy with his Dozer Operators.

It had been a joyful holiday with the children and with Sally Spaniel as a stimulator. The boys had grown strong, had arrived white and sallow and boarded the plane back to school looking as brown as berries. Caroline, now 18, took a job in the ladies' dress shop in Luanshya. We were now firmly established in the Zambian Copperbelt but with no connection to the heavy metal.

"Dad, look what I got with my catty."

Turaco

Field training.   The Dumpy Level.

CHAPTER TWO

1968/1969

1968

This whole year was to be devoted to something that I had never done in my life before, building seven earth dams on the government ranch plus studiously learning how to do so from my Rhodesian Guide Book. I was provided the bulldozers, scrapers and compacters by CWA, [Conex Working Account], a heavy plant unit owned and capitalised by the government to enable a boost to food production. The management and staff were from the private sector and the Unit had to finance its running costs by charging for its services. Since it was capitalised by government, CWA could charge much lower operational fees than private sector contractors, but it had to confine itself to the agricultural and forestry sector.

All the dams I built, ultimately 'held' and some were very large in their capacity. One was, later, my own design for cheapness, I called it my maverick contour dam, suitable for high upper catchment areas like Miengwe, built with one bulldozer and no spillway; maverick = 'not according to the book'. The procedure was to clear-off the topsoil following a contour line pegged out by one of my 'lads' with his Dumpy Level. Then pile a huge bank of impervious sub-soil, six feet high. This enabled small village communities to utilise hill top soils without needing to walk miles for water.

In 1968 I bought a new short wheel based Land Rover on a government loan, made in Ndola! For only £948, I was ready for 'bush whacking'. I was better equipped for the rough roads of Ndola Rural District than with Jo's topless MGB, one of the gorgeous old originals that we loved. So we were off to explore the vast country to the South of the Copperbelt cities, controlled by the various chiefdoms. Sally Spaniel, whom we had brought with us from Tanzania, loved the wind in her flapping ears in the open back of my new Land Rover. We found a vast area of grassland in Chief Lesa's area known as Mpongwe. Usually flat treeless open country signifies flood plain but in this case the land was dry despite 70 inches of recent rainfall. Thus I realised that this was a vast area of limestone beds beneath a fertile soil. It looked promising for an irrigation scheme with boreholes, probably, given a massive financial investment of course, however no-one would invest in Chiefs' land however; one for the future?

"Wake up, we're here again"   1968

DAM CONSTUCTION

I set about my concept of resettling Chief Nkambo's village people on family farms of fifteen acres who were traditional 'shifting cultivators'. This traditional survival system which covers the whole of northern Zambia is to cut down the trees and burn them for the ash to fertilise the crops for a few years and then to move to another area when the soil is exhausted. This survival regime prevents the government from providing schools, clinics and water wells etc. My idea was to provide them with an opportunity to settle on a fertile soil area on 15 acre family farms with modern agricultural techniques and inputs and to produce cash crops. I had always found that providing hefty loans or indeed Aid, created dependency rather than initiative, so the plan would not be dependent upon loans. The Israelis did not agree with this and they created huge co-operatives near Luanshya for larger numbers of people, mainly unemployed youth, from townships. Loan finance was enormous. This was **Kafulafuta.**

I visited Chief Nkambo to proffer my idea of resettling his people on more fertile land in an area called **Miengwe**. He was very shy and fearful of losing his authority with government staff organising everything. I emphasised that there would be no compulsion to join, and the final decision would be his. We would call a meeting and explain the details to everybody.

Zambia's three and half million people had no reason to go hungry with land the size of Europe and yet the threat of closed borders to Rhodesia had already created a maize shortage and a plea for Aid. A whole change of attitude was called for by Zambia's politicians. A Green Revolution was now the clarion call. However with copper mining where the money was, no one wanted to return to the axe and the hoe, even though the land was free. So, commercial agriculture had to be 'on the cards' also in addition to community development.

Some figures appeared in the local press to frighten people into taking notice of the politicians' call to grow more food; "It took two million years for the world population to grow to 1 billion, but it will take only 27 years for the population to grow to 7 billion; starvation threatens."

Here are some examples of my labourers intriguing names; Lonti Kapefu, John Mulikinta, Washington Beans, Simon Kapofu, Simoni Mivebela, Takison Chile, Julius Mabwe, Letis Mwape, Robert James Mawaga, Levi Ngoma (our Kapitao).

Flying squirrel in Miengwe

Luanshya - Kafulafuta

Our daughter Caroline married Iain on 7th September 1968 in Mombasa at the age of 19. We conceded one year of the two we had demanded for the lovers to wait. Hence we all went off to Mombasa for a grand holiday. We visited the old Fort and Philip picked up on the history of Mombasa. He loved adventure. He was telling us "Turkish pirates took over the island of Mombasa, like they did the Toten Island in Tanga Bay in Tanzania in 1588. Then a cannibal tribe from south of the Zambezi called Zimba, ate their way up the coast to Mombasa and then ate the Turks. In 1591 the Portuguese arrived and built this Fort. They were later driven out by the Sultan of Zanzibar."

Mombasa wedding

Bride's brothers

Wow! A wedding in Mombasa

After the wedding we took off for Kenya Safari Club with the bride and groom followed by Tsavo Park, the Momella Game Reserve, and finally the coastal palm fringed beach of the Mnarani Club, together with the bride and groom! Well, she was a bit young. She was following her mother's example, who also married aged 19 years. We didn't have a leg to stand on really.

Tsavo 1968

Tsavo

Back in Luanshya, Jo and I and the boys were entertained one evening in Luanshya by the Gay Desperadoes. This West Indian band playing 'oil drums' were magnificent; so polished, and with a comprehensive programme of sheer joyful rhythm. We spoke to one of the instrumentalists who said they couldn't read a note of musical script. That immense sense of rhythm and excitement is genetic with the black races and something that I thought we might come to enjoy increasingly in the Western World.

Finally our exploration of Ndola Rural District led us, with Robert Taylor, 75 miles south to the Kafue River and a hand propelled ferry to the land of another tribe. Jo and I were ceremonially greeted by a rather beau character, with a handle-bar moustache and a smart London suit, Senior Chief Machiya. His people thrived on fish and game meat, but as he explained, copper miners were crossing the river to the north with boats and modern weapons and killing all his game. He wondered; "Since you are a Government Officer, can you do anything about that?" I responded, "I will have a damn good try." And so the Machiya Game Management Area No. 23 concept was born.

(End 1968)

Brian   Jo   Robert   Taylor   Phil

Machiya ferry

Luscambo Malipila,
ferry man.

24

1969

19th January 1969

I had been visiting Mufulira Ranch almost daily. In January I had taken our son Philip, aged 13 years, along. He loved the challenge of camping out in the wilds. Unfortunately the Christmas school holiday had coincided with the rainy season and we were caught by a massive storm with a fireworks display in the sky and soaking wet beds, not to mention being the evening meal for the mosquito fraternity, but he was not deterred. Fortunately, my wish to encourage my offspring to enjoy wild places was restored by the next day being very hot. We trekked through woodland to my first completed C.A.3 dam and found a flock of black ducks to exercise Philip's marksmanship in aid of an evening meal. We swam in the reservoir and then got lost trekking back to my Land Rover. Not only a black duck but a black mark for Dad! Back in Luanshya, we all went to the cinema to see *'The Jungle Book'*.

Elvis successfully regained his position at the top of the Pop-charts by getting away from films and getting back onto the stage, having had his nose put-out somewhat by the Beatles.

Sadly, after the Christmas holiday we saw our two boys off back to England and boarding school, by BOAC VC10. These separations were always traumatic, leaving us questioning our parental wisdom.

After our boys had flown back to school I was invited to a Conference in Lusaka. I drove the 200 miles in Jo's topless MGB., with the wind in my hair, feeling happily in control.

Eminent members were:

Norman Beaumont	Director of Rural Development
Merfyn Temple	International anti-apartheid figure
Mr Mumeko	Zambian Government
Mr Guy Clutton-Brock.	Farmer with wife, from Rhodesia
Rev. Michael Scott	Human Rights campaigner
Major Peter Moxon	Commercial Farmer in the Copperbelt
H Pattison	S.I.D.A., Swedish International Development Agency.

The latter gentleman offered me four Swedish volunteers. I was really happy at the outcome of this discussion and Councillor Mumeko was tremendously enthusiastic about the Miengwe plan. Apparently he had recently returned from Cuba. He was quite a left-wing politician and of some considerable authority, I was told.

Phil. camping out, Mufulira Ranch.

Christmas toys.

Jo and I enjoyed meeting up with an expatriate large scale pig farmer named Vorster. We were pig farmers in England in our days of yore after WWII, and were besotted pig lovers. There was a good market for pig meat now that the Zambians had adopted a European diet, hence my wish to get our family farmers at Miengwe and Kafulafuta into pig keeping. Mr Vorster was selling 66,000 kwacha worth of pork per year. (1 kwacha = 50 pence).

We now had an Irish family managing my 'heavy plant' Caterpillar equipment from CWA. Paddy and Della Prendergast had become good friends. They were an ideal foil for Jo in her unbridled sense of humour. The next job was to be forest clearing, partly in Miengwe area in preparation for my settlement scheme and partly for the Forestry Department Plantations managed by Chris Davis. This very efficient unit consisted of two giant Caterpillar D7 bulldozers attached to each end of a ship's anchor chain to fell the trees into windrows followed by two smaller Caterpillar D6's, with stingers, to prod the laggards.

Clearing 100 acres was heavy work and after a twelve hour day, Paddy returned home to Ndola, exhausted enough to do justice to his trolley of beer bottles packed on the top shelf, demanding to be emptied down Paddy's throat and subsequently to reside on the lower shelf in weightless emptiness. The household awaited the conclusion of this daily ritual before proceeding to supper with guests. Paddy enjoyed a D7 capacity.

Pigs   *Brian's design for the Israelis*

Ships' anchor chain windrowing trees

This Irishman coincidentally lived in Killarney Road. At their house, we met a man who owned a Company that was well-known for heavy duty land clearing, named Barkley Kay. His rise to success with Caterpillar heavy plant resulted from the failed Groundnut Scheme in Tanganyika in 1948. Many local people benefitted from this misconceived scheme to yield margarine for the starving British, but it cost the taxpayers £1.2 billion in today's money. The vast area selected for growing groundnuts had never before been cropped because rainfall was too low. The local village headmen could have advised the ministry eggheads in London that the selected area was too dry for crops, but they wisely kept stum and profited from years of employment at UK tax payer's expense. The village headmen had a knack of surviving, like the Labour Government.

Another interesting elderly character we met enjoying Paddy's *bonhomie* personality was Westergaard. This man fought with his fellow Rhodesians against the Germans in Deutsch Ostafrika later to become Tanganyika. He spoke highly of the German General Von Lettow-Vorbeck who treated British prisoners with respect and "was a very competent foe". On the British side, the famous South African General Jan Smuts he said "used to visit the aforesaid General in Germany at the time to get to know his enemy better". He also told us about the Gold Rush in Rhodesia after WWI. "After a year's mining, a miner he knew would slap £800 on the bar in Salisbury and ask the proprietor to let him know when it had all gone, and then went off on a three month long binge. Everyone was scrupulously honest in those days."

Jo, at this time, secured a job with the fancy goods store in Luanshya, owned by Jaz Solanki. The store was known as Solanki's Store. She was employed as the part-time window dresser, and became very popular with the Solanki family She increased their trade such that she was invited to organise the owner's Indian wedding reception in the biggest hotel in the Copperbelt, in Kitwe city. Who better, with her love of theatre, to stage a major event with glamour and panache, than Jo Dawtrey? The papers were subsequently full of it. This was 1st February 1969. There were 250 guests. The African waiters were of the Dorchester Hotel standard and the food included a whole, huge salmon from Scotland with a massive block of carved ice. Jo and I resided at the head of the table next to the bridegroom. Jaz's new wife's name was Lamella, a lovely Indian girl, somewhat over-whelmed by it all. Jo and I happily danced the night away over a week-end, reminding us of our heady nights in the tropical ocean resort of Tanga, Tanzania.

Jo organised Solanki wedding reception in Kitwe

Solanki store Luanshya

February 1969
Heavy rains continued. My dams were all full and holding. These remote ranch dams attracted two nude swimmers, guess who! The best photos of my achievement at dam building all have a celebrated naked lady in them so they have had to be confined to my album. We hadn't had so much fun without our clothes on for years.

The Government was now making an effort to make Zambians less dependent upon the racialist south for food. New office hours were extended to 8.00 am through to 5.00 pm. Imported goods were to carry 50% duty and most other shop goods to carry 30% duty to raise revenue. I would be looking for my employer, the Government, to fund my family farming schemes including boreholes to ensure clean water, and 'self-help school' teachers, and the standard Rural Health Centre staff, both of which required long term investment.

On this latter point, I was faced with the need to secure the confidence, as a white man, of the chiefs in the rural district in addition to the African political hierarchy of the Province. At this moment, I was faced with the problem of rising antagonism by the Senior Chief Mushili. Newsmen were harassing me, unfortunately, and 'fake news' kept appearing in the national press about Brian Dawtrey. It was all about the authority of chiefs being threatened and villagers being cajoled into moving against their will by a British Aid worker.

Our good friend Robert Taylor, Farm Management Officer had, possibly, under my influence, as Honorary Game Warden in Tanzania and now in Zambia, decided to change course and become a 'white hunter'. We had many exciting adventures into places in the extreme north west of the province, in the forested upper reaches of the Kafue River where elephants roamed. Robert and his girlfriend flying doctor nurse June had really 'clicked' and loved these bush adventures. In the evenings with them a theatrical scene emerged in our house, with Jo's merry influence, leading to many hilarious evenings. Robert was good at impersonations which always set Jo off playing a role. Our two boys, when home, contributed on piano, guitar and the *Afzelia quanzensis* tree big seed pod rattles. These one and a half foot long pods made great rhythmic rattles. Our new Telefunken 5090 record player stirred the dust.

Robert Taylor   *elephant hunter with a .22 rifle*

School hols 1969 with Robert Tayor and June

No.46 in Itawa Ndola

We were digging-ourselves-in as they say. I was promoted to Provincial Land Planning Officer in the Provincial Offices in Ndola with a wonderful extensive house and garden being provided for us by the government in Itawa Ndola.

The guerrilla campaign in Portuguese East Africa which became Mozambique was dealt a severe blow by the murder of their leader, Dr Mondlane in Dar es Salaam. It was said that his own fellow guerrillas who were trained in Tanzania, organised his demise because he had a white American wife. So we were surrounded by wars and strife. What was it that the famous Victorian explorer Richard Burton said; "Peace is the dream of the wise, war is the history of Man." The strong anti-American feeling in East Africa arose from their experience with J.F.Kennedy's 'vassals' the Peace Corps whom were rightly or wrongly thought to be American "neo-colonialists", with their trunks full of books on US history and their preaching about the "Finest democracy in the world" and, "we're just like you", behaviour.

The Lamba People

Chief Nkambo's people now faced a step up from the past into a settled life on a 15 acre farms, reliant upon an element of science and trade. The project was officially named the <u>Miengwe Village Regrouping Scheme.</u> The people of Chief Nkambo and the surrounding area were Lamba by tribe. They still clung to their ancient culture, unlike the copper miners who hailed from tribes all over Zambia and had been 'modernised' to some extent. Chief Nkambo's people had not suffered destruction of their traditional culture by missionary zeal. When Jo canvassed a mission in Ndola to assist with the Women's Club she was visiting, they refused because they "are not Christians".

Jo and I became involved in studies of the past culture of these people. How did the chief view justice? He explained to us their principle of justice; compensating the victim of a crime as the primary consideration before the punishment of the guilty. He quoted a case of a young man who stole a cow, had it slaughtered and sold the meat in the township. He was condemned to work as a slave for the offended family for five years.

Witchcraft, we were told, acted as a pressure valve for taught nerves and emotions in society thus avoiding aggression. He didn't mention the suffering of selected victims. There was probably a connection between the prevalent mistrust that exists between fellow Africans and the prevalence of witchcraft.

The Lamba Chief's court called witnesses. The elders and Councillors listened to all sides and took a considered view, like a jury, upon which the

Chief decided the punishment. Capital punishment was doled out for incest, witchcraft, murder but not manslaughter or rape.

There were no sexual relations between man and wife during the nursing of the baby, which was usually for two to three years, hence the high level of adultery. Divorce and adultery seemed to be very common but the strength of kinship pervaded greater than family strength. Lines of inheritance and kinship were stronger between uncle and nephew than between father and son. This group dependence, rather than the British ethic of individual responsibility, explained why my African senior staff always seemed to lack a sense of individual responsibility.

Anyone who stepped out of line, or who was unpopular, or was very old, was branded an *imfwiti* and cast out into the forest to live alone, which was not really possible. This tended to stifle initiative, out of fear. Stories of meeting *imfwiti* in the forest were legion. A man with one leg leaping along the path, usually naked, in the dark shadows 'like a wizard' who carried poisoned darts. A white wizard was labelled an *umulaye*. A prominent hill exists in Miengwe named Petamikwa. The Chief advised us that his people never climbed that hill for fear of *imfwiti*, goblins, ogres, demons, witches and 'little people'.

Petamikwa Hill

15 acre farmstead on fertile soils, Miengwe.

Jo.

On Petamikwa Hill

Throughout the whole of Africa, the belief in spiritual survival has always been paramount. After death those ancestral spirits become an active ingredient in the welfare of African society. Some tribes accepted their ancestral spirits resided in some prominent geographical feature or mighty trees in their locality. Petamikwa Hill was the lair of Lamba ancestral spirits. It was also said that a huge snake lived in a rock cavity at the peak as a guardian against human trespass. No Lamba person had ever set foot on that hill, though I did find red rock paintings there, obviously pre-Bantu.

Traditional African culture makes mankind's minds subject directly to the supervision of their ancestral spirits. Religion on the other hand, via the church and its missionaries, gather human spirits together under the auspices of one God, and that God exercises authority over society via a Head of the Church or a senior 'cleric'.

Well; here were two little people that loved climbing Petamikwa Hill over the years, in absolute privacy!

Ownership of property in Africa was unknown and control of land-use was exercised by hierarchy. I did not visualise a problem here with settled family farmers being self-supporting, using their personal initiative, but the Senior Chief Mushili was persistently resistant this idea which was to be a major challenge for me.

"Brian; what are you are taking on to your shoulders with this Miengwe Scheme? I think you are delving into African culture too much. You are planning a social change for Chief Nkambo's people. This is quite political. Be careful. You might get labelled an *umulaye*. Look what happened in Tanzania when we tried to leave; the government refused to pay our air fares home."

"Ah, that was different; there was no British Embassy, we had no protection. President Nyerere expelled the Embassy because Margaret Thatcher declined to make sanctions against the Apartheid Regime. We are all good friends here. We are guests, helping the rural folk, the Mums and Dads in the rural areas to enjoy an upgrade in their standard of living. Also I am not forcing anyone to join, it's up to them. That's the difference to what the Vorster government did in Soweto."

I was preparing for an onslaught on the District Development Committee in an effort to gain support for Miengwe Scheme. I succeeded in getting the District Governor's signature requesting 23,000 kwacha, which is £11,500. I would present this to the Provincial Minister in Ndola. I later addressed the Rural Development sub-committee in H.Q. Lusaka. Bob McCorkle and Mr Mumeko supported me.

3rd March 1969

I received a message from O.N.D.P. Lusaka, the Office of National Development Projects, saying that funds for Miengwe were not allowed. Whereupon I wrote an irate letter to the Permanent Secretary, via N.Beaumont, copied it around the political arena, and retired to bed.

17th March 1969

I attended a vital meeting of the Provincial Development Committee Executive in Ndola. All the Copperbelt District Governors were present as well as an O.N.D.P. representative, Mr Ling from the Ministry of Finance. I delivered my somewhat philosophical oratory on rural development in general and then mentioned the local example, Miengwe Village Regrouping Scheme. There was overwhelming support from the District Governors. The case went to the Vice President for a final decision which would overrule the O.N.D.P. I had met the Vice President in Kafulafuta Israeli Scheme area, when as always, Jo got him into fits of giggles.

Our two boys were sitting mock G.C.S.E. Richard got six passes despite the disadvantage of his African Primary education at Arusha School in Tanzania, where he studied Kiswahili, nature studies (his top subject) and the geography and history of Tanzania.

A great friend, Ben Van de Poll from our department in Lusaka H.Q. came up to see my work, bush clearing, dam building, etc. He would later recommend my skills to the World Bank in 1977 when my contract was due to end with Zambia.

I awaited news of finance for the Miengwe plan. Meanwhile, I was reading historic records of the Copperbelt by an early explorer named C.M.Doke in 1904. On the subject of the country he called Ilamba, he said it was heavily populated by wildlife to the extent that he had "no problem of shooting antelope for breakfast." He counted fourteen species of animals on the Kafue River flats in the Ndola Rural District. He recorded animals such as lion, hyena, vultures, lechwe, leopard, hippos. Today, sadly, there are no wild animals in the Province apart from elephants in the far North West forest in the Kafue River headwaters and in Senior Chief Machiya's area 150 miles to the south west beyond the Kafue River.

Contour dam depth 12 ft

Ensuant upon my lecture to Robert Taylor that I would never shoot a zebra, etc., etc., I had a heavy experience, or was it a dream? Robert and I were sleeping in our standard issue bell tent, in Ndubeni, wherein the Kafue flats lie. I was awakened by a herd of hippos grazing around our tent. Then I saw a zebra in the tall grass on its own. I told Robert to sit down and leave it alone. However, it sprang through our open doorway and flattened me on the floor. I imagined it had a lion's face and legs and a zebra skin. It was definitely a lion. I shouted for my rifle as the lion got me by the throat. I managed to get the muzzle under its jaw and squeezed the trigger. The animal dropped dead on top of me. I swore that I would never let a zebra pass me by again, much to Robert's amusement.

At this time I was on my own as an Honorary Wildlife Ranger with some support from the Wildlife Conservation Society of Zambia, hence merely checking traders on the streets in Ndola for skins, captured monkeys and game meat coming in from neighbouring provinces. I had full powers of arrest and confiscation of vehicles and weapons and entry into private houses of suspects, unlike game keepers in England. The African Cambridge educated Commissioner of Forestry was heard advising his staff, "Watch out for that man Dawtrey, he's dangerous." I became suspicious of Forestry Junior staff and found one with 'bush meat' in his house in the Forest Reserve. I also, sadly, had to apprehend a trader on the river bridge in town selling wild ducks with their wings broken to keep them fresh whilst trading. How else can one keep the meat fresh with no fridge?

Jo expressed the view that this kind of activity might get me into trouble with the senior Zambian hierarchy and probably did little to save wildlife. "A much more concerted organisation would be required with local African Rangers as back up." We decided, long term, that we would work towards that goal.

Jo had been desperate to see our two sons for their Easter holidays for which they were not entitled an airfare. She had saved £260 as a window dresser for Solanki's and had told the boys that it was for them to fly out, "but it wasn't enough". Richard wrote from school and said, "Never mind Mum, you can save that £260 towards my future career." He meant his plan to buy a VW car in Zambia. Jo decided to go to Mombasa instead to see Caroline, now married. Jo would never overcome her regret of being separated from her children. After her three weeks away, I received a picture card of Mombasa and the romantic tropical beaches nearby. She talked of a ship's captain whirling her round on the deck in a 'blast' on board ship. He dropped her and cracked her coccyx. " I'm coming home next week".

We realised that three weeks separation was the outside limit that we could tolerate apart. As teenage lovers, our immature brains finally grew together into maturity and to some extent we were inseparable. The Royal Geographical Society, of which I was a Fellow, sent me a diary extract of the wife of the Victorian explorer R.F. Burton, 1861. She wrote 14 points ensuring a happy marriage.

"Point 1 - Let your husband find you a companion, friend and advisor, also a confidante, that he might miss nothing at home and let him find in his wife what he and many other men, thinks is only to be found in a mistress, that he might seek nothing outside his home." I understood that. Also "Point 5 - Be prepared at any moment to follow him at an hour's notice and rough it like a man." Jo qualified. "Point 14: - Keep everything going and let nothing be at a standstill." That was Jo.

May 1969

Adding to my political affiliations, I met with Ruben Kamanga, the Minister of Rural Development and spent a whole day showing him our scheme near Chingola for settling ex-Kalulushi Farm College graduates on irrigated family farms on State Land. This small scheme was quite impressive as a result of them being trained to grow vegetables for the blossoming Kitwe City market. It was called Ipafu Settlement Scheme. Robert Taylor came too hence we ended the day at a Flying Doctor Service Party with June. The round trip was 164 miles in Robert's Ford Cortina. He complained about a noise in the back end of his car. Upon investigation, I found an absence of oil in the differential. Also we found the shock absorbers were shot, due to having Michelin tyres which were heavy. "Robert, bush-whacking after game in a Cortina can be expensive."

Jo and I later spent a jolly day touring the projects with guests: Officialdom from Lusaka; Iain Gordon, Chief Livestock Officer, Norman Beaumont Director of Rural Development, Richard Hedges, Provincial Livestock Officer (who later became a Secretary to the National Farmers Union in Dorset, England) and Robert Taylor, Farm Management Officer. We visited the Israeli hated pig unit at Kafulafuta co-operative farm. The unit building cost only £200 for six pens. A poultry unit had also been set up – battery cages – outdoors!

Outdoor hen batteries *Anderson Mucha*

Robert had some leave due, so he decided upon a holiday in the highly civilised and prosperous country of Rhodesia. "You need a haircut Robert," Jo said over supper. His hair was down below his ears and black. "You'll get arrested as a guerrilla suspect." We took two inches off al-round in the name of U.D.I.

Robert aspired to branch out into a wider world, a more exciting world, a wild world, as indeed I had done as an ex farm manager of a Norfolk farm going off to 'darkest Africa' with the family. The exciting story I told in my recent book *Going Places.* In our Norfolk days we lived quite near to Wheat-fen Broad where the famous naturalist Ted Ellis and his wife Phyllis lived, literally, amongst the reeds. Ted used to talk about "rich adventures" in wildlife. Apparently Robert's uncle was a well known personality, also living amongst the reeds on the Broads. He made his living as a river bailiff. This spirit of 'rich adventures' took Robert, many years later, to Rhodesia where he built a house on his own game reserve with a great variety of wild animals He and his wife Margaret later suffered the misfortune to be the victims of 'Mad Mugabe' and his Army, who marched in and confiscated the property and all the wild animals, including his rhino.

News came through from Lusaka after the Budget, that the requested funds for Miengwe would be included in the Provincial Allocation. This was a Red Letter Day in our lives; little me and less little Jo had succeeded in opening the government purse. This was entirely due to the Jo 'clicking' with the Deputy President, Simon Kapwepwe, on that Kafulafuta field day leading to him over-riding all the opposition in the Cabinet. So it was full steam ahead'. The next task was persuading scattered villagers to join, after the drilling of boreholes for water and pegging out 15 acre farms. I welcomed the Swedish Volunteers who were to set about building themselves a house.

Everest Siame persuading the people to join

Senior Chief Mushili with his Joker

Matters came to a head with Senior Chief Mushili. He played upon the village headmen's natural fear of a change in their status as leaders in their village communities when many villages would be submerged into a group. A vote was taken at a tribal gathering of about a hundred headmen. Only fifteen voted to join the Scheme. Some wives stood up and declared that they were joining despite what their husbands said. Chief Mushili declared to the gathering of newspaper reporters that villagers were to be dragooned into joining against their will. This became a national scandal reminiscent of the international news event of a few years ago of 500,000 Tonga people of the Gwembe Valley being forcibly evicted from their tribal lands by armed police resulting in outright war, spears against guns. That event attracted T.V. cameras from the world media. However, in those colonial times, a man named Sir Roy Welensky ruled the Federation of States, Northern and Southern Rhodesia and Nyasaland and his policy was economy first, people second. A contract had been let to Italy to build Kariba Dam which would supply 'green' electricity to the Copperbelt and the farmers in South Rhodesia and Nyasaland; now Malawi. The Gwembe valley was to become a vast lake behind the now famous Kariba Dam.

The Minister for Rural Development pointed out that, "Chief Nkambo had consented to Mr Dawtrey's survey and has supported his plan to bring modern facilities to the benefit of his people and there would be no compulsion by Zambia Government." He also said, "The Copperbelt Provincial Development Committee has recommended the plan for 250 families.

During this spell covered by the Times of Zambia newspaper, the British High Commission contacted me offering immediate flights for me and my family back to London. I declined of course. It was "just a temporary blip" I reassured them. What worried Jo throughout this period was the high prevalence of witchcraft in Lamba country. I considered that since I was not prone to fear, upon witchcraft depends for its success, I was immune. Lack of education was something that would be overcome eventually at Miengwe.

President Kaunda subsequently offered the people 50 free corrugated iron sheets for anyone who built himself a sound mud-brick house at Miengwe. The villagers voted to join the Scheme by the time my home leave was due in 1970. I had, by that time built one of my contour dams in the valley nearby in case of a borehole pump failure.

It was the end of my Contract with Zambia Government in August, and they requested renewal so off we went on three months leave, via VC10 to Gatwick, London, to gather up our children and stay in a hired ancient cottage at Cley-next-the-Sea in Norfolk, a fabulous location surrounded by wild nature reserves along the foreshore. Richard said "Look, Gypy Geese." Egyptian *Geese* he was right; "*home from home*".

CHAPTER THREE

1970

12th November 1970

We arrived back in Lusaka at 10.30 pm by Air Malawi. The airline found us a double room at the Ridgeway Hotel. It was very hot; suicide month. We ordered cold lemonade to be brought to the room and it was! Things were looking up in Zambia.

The next day we reported to my boss in Lusaka, Norman Beaumont, and were told, "Just carry on where you left off three months ago Brian. A promising young Planning Officer named Geoff White has kept everything going, but you'll have to look out for the new Zambian Provincial Agricultural Officer named Chikoti. He is into, what you might call, the more traditional African way of doing things."

After a glorious afternoon by the swimming pool recovering from freezing foggy Britain, we took off for Ndola in a new Hawker Siddeley 125 rear mounted jet, only to land again with a hydraulic fault. Four hours later, we took off again apprehensively, in an obviously overloaded plane, arriving in Ndola at 10.30 pm. Our friends and house guests, Gerald and Pat Pennington met us. We managed to dodge Customs and arrived home at No. 7, now Kafue Drive (ex-Ennerdale Drive), to find our house as we left it, with Sally Spaniel. Oddly, she was not quite sure who we were at first and had forgotten a bit of our doggy language or it could have been the intense heat that was getting her down; she had a fine black coat. Our old MGB was all polished up ready for happy hours. With its electric overdrive switched on, it could do 'the ton' with the roof off on the Copperbelt inter-city tar roads. It was such a joy being topless for six months. It was an 'old' model with a strut down the centre of the windscreen and 100% chrome bumpers and spoke wheels with a wing nut.

We shed most of our U.K. clothing the next day in the bright sunshine and settled to the slower pace of life in Zambia. We had found life in Britain grim, with strikers ruling the country. The brighter side of the gloom was the uprising of popular music; all songs with a romantic message in those days. We bought lots of L.P.'s to play on our three-speaker Telefunken 5090 stereo record player, including Petula Clark singing her beautiful song *Downtown,* and Paul Mauriat's well known *Love is Blue* and of course the latest tropical Pop songs from South Africa; *The Lion Sleeps Tonight* and Bert Kaempfert's wonderful trumpets doing *African Safari, Whimoway,* which everyone was mad about. It seemed strange how disconnected these two worlds were, we hardly seemed to have been away.

We went over to see Bella and Paddy Prendergast and their "little delight" Pam, to whom we gave a gorgeous doll from England. They had been quite worried about our late arrival yesterday, afraid we might have been hijacked. The Irish knew about that sort of thing. We enjoyed a laugh with a traditional cold beer or three, and finally organised a trip to look at 'the job' on the morrow.

At our offices, I met our new Zambian Provincial Agricultural Officer named Joshua Chikoti. He welcomed me politely and I noticed a character sitting in the corner dressed in tribal clothes instead of the usual western suit worn by all office staff in Zambia. I later learned that this was his doctor/advisor with whom he frequently consulted on matters of official business, probably including the handling of the new Provincial Land Planning Officer, me, whom was not under his technical control, being in the new Department of Rural Development. Nevertheless, Chikoti was required to support me administratively – staff wages, camping allowances, petrol, transport, drawing office, typist, hence plenty of scope for him to exercise his status in competition with Norman Beaumont.

Miengwe Scheme was running OK Geoff White told me, and the Swedish volunteers, Gothe Alexson, Anders Linden, Lennart Granath and Peter Borg were happy and busy. Geoff White had found them a government truck to procure inputs and for marketing farmers' produce. Crop husbandry advice from Lennart Granath was producing some wonderful crops of maize from the fertile red soils. The first settler families even had access to water from a communal tap, a revolution in itself. Peter Borg was in charge and doing an impressive job. Their new self-built Swedish house was attracting riotous weekends with the Swedish community in Ndola. Interestingly, this traditional design was similar to the 16th Century Mary Arden's house preserved in Wilmcote, Stratford-upon-Avon. Upstairs was open-plan shelving for visitors to sleep, in this case rather than children, with a downstairs open to the roof space for feasting, drinking and everything else that Swedes do communally. There were three rooms on the lower floor; kitchen, one bedroom and dressing/wash room. Indeed a "merry place".

I had been able to procure a brick making machine from the United Nations which design came from South America. This was a simple hand-operated pressure device for turning a mixture of the local clay laterite (which contains ferrous gravel or 'murram') and cement into durable sun dried building blocks. Cement was produced in Zambia and the resultant blocks had been approved by the Power and Works Department, P.W.D., for building single storey houses.

I had to attend the monthly round of Provincial Development Committee, P.D.C. meetings, under the chairmanship of the Minister of State for the Copperbelt Province, Mr Bulawayo. Present were the chiefs, district governors, provincial heads and Mr Storrs the Director of Forestry. The Agenda indicated that the serious business was to be the land dispute between certain chiefs whose land was to be 'acquired' by Forestry Department for tree planting, not just any old land but the best of the food producing soils. The Forestry Department had, under colonial rule, become a major power in the province because of the need for charcoal and timber for the copper mines. The acquisition of more land for tree planting was brewing up to be the cause of major conflicts because of growing food shortages. This was my province.

Every meeting opened with a fine rendering of the National Anthem which over many years of attendance became ingrained into my psyche: Music by Enoch Sontonga 1897; used in Tanzania and RSA also:

Verse One	**Chorus**
Stand and sing of Zambia,	Praise be to God,
Proud and free,	Praise be, praise be, praise be,
Land of work and joy in unity.	Bless our great nation,
Victors in the struggle for the right,	Zambia, Zambia, Zambia
We have won freedoms fight.	Free men we stand,
All one strong and free.	Under the flag of our land

There are two more, lengthy, verses which I will not burden my readers with. Oratory was impressive from all sides, as usual, condemning the Forestry Department. However, in the outcome the Minister approved it, adding that he would find more fertile land for the people, and provide advice on modern methods of increasing yields. He meant *Brian Dawtrey would*.

'God' seems to have imbued Africans with a natural gift for oratory, as well as rhythm, not to mention, a substantial capacity for alcohol. Furthermore, 'God' has also endowed Zambia with giant termitaria ['ant hills'] from the top of which to platform their oratory talent to a crowded outdoor theatre of peasantry. A few corrugated iron sheets were provided above for shade, for the privileged that is. The audience were condemned to sit out in the baking sun for hours, imbibing the wisdom in silent scepticism.

Friday was yet another meeting, this time the Ndola Rural District Committee, basically to discuss how we could develop the Mpongwe area further south. Mpongwe was another vast unutilised fertile area with huge potential for irrigated crops. The Chairman, Daniel Chintilye, had a farm near Miengwe and was an educated, active supporter of individual enterprise as opposed to the traditional tribal fears of witchcraft against people who defied the communal ethic.

I had attended so many meetings with the African elite that I was becoming well known, despite being of the hated white image. Having overcome the Senior Chief Mushili debacle, I seemed to have the full support of the Zambian politicians at provincial level and even of the Vice President. This was in no small measure due to Jo's effervescent personality, putting Africans at ease when we met informally. That element of trust was so vital in putting-over new schemes of agricultural development in that young nation.

3rd November 1970

I jumped into our MGB at dawn and drove off on tar roads to Kitwe city and beyond to the Kalulushi area and from there, turning south into Chief Mukutuma's villages. This was official business about the Forestry Department's acquisition of the Chief's Native Land for forestry plantations. We grew to be a substantial band of officials and The Press, the villagers became angry. An attack was made on the Forest Guards with sticks and stones. Fortunately I was among government 'heavyweights' who administered lengthy oratory of a political nature thus calming the fear of the people. We ended up singing the National Anthem and relaxed for a friendly exchange with the village headmen. One of them offered me a bucket of emerald bearing rocks for 10 kwacha (£5). There was going to be an emerald mine there one day; Zambian Emeralds.

25th November 1970

The Swedish Embassy had phoned me requesting a public meeting at Miengwe scheme; hence there we were with Chikoti in the 'ant hill' chair. I was supposed to chair the gathering of Lamba people but fortunately I had laryngitis, hence Chikoti was able to assert his new found status before the chiefs, Swedish guests and the four Swedish SIDA [Swedish International Development Agency] Volunteers.

The Scheme had made great strides during my leave. There was now a substantial area of cleared land, a reasonable gravel road, some good houses, a Health Centre and a functioning borehole. Chikoti spoke very well and was translated into Lamba by Daniel Chintilye. The Swedish volunteers were working very hard and were of good practical skills. They spoke good English of course as did all the Swedish community in Ndola. We enjoyed a much civilised tea in the Swedes' house after the formalities ended and Jo read out a skittish poem she had written about Peter Borg and 'his boys', which caused great hilarity.

28th November 1970

There was another field meeting, this time near Kitwe but on Chief Nkana's land south of the city. This land-use plan was to move villagers out and set up an irrigation scheme to grow vegetables for Kitwe city. The villagers were to undergo training and be allocated each their own plot. The United Nations had come in to manage the scheme called Chapula. As usual, I was the only white face at this tribal gathering. Boundaries were agreed and government financial backing requested, to be supplemented by the U.N. I was elected to the management committee, doubtless to act as the official football! It had been quite a fortnight for a start of my three year contract! In June 2017, I sat down to lunch in England with French beans from Kitwe, Zambia on the label. They were a bit stringy.

December 1970

I spent a whole week organising my drawing office and stores. Chaos prevailed, however my now seventeen junior staff were all happily prepared to get out into the bush with their field surveying equipment and soil augers, despite the inconvenience of camp life. They received a camping allowance for that, Chikoti permitting. My new Junior Technical Officer, named Pongolati, was a School Certificate graduate with post graduate survey training. I found it frustrating trying to arouse any enthusiasm from him for the field work. I had always found the ex-Primary School level Africans to be the best workers and the most reliable enthusiasts for the political 'Agrarian Revolution.'

We saw a film with the Penningtons who were lodging with us, called *"Five Man Army"*, an unpromising title but which turned out to be a 'trump card' in a criminal minded world. Criminal acts committed with aplomb, were always greeted with loud applause by the Africans in the stalls and they were thoroughly enjoyed by us too. Come to think of it, Adolf Hitler rose to power on the back of the mass acclaim for his criminal acts committed with aplomb.

Jo and I made a lucky purchase of a Peugeot 204 for 1000 kwacha, which is £500. The old chap who sold it to us had been knocking back double whiskies all day. We sold our Land Rover to pay for it. The market price was 1,840 Kwacha. The MGB was unsuitable for the gravel rutted roads in Ndola Rural, especially with the very heavy rainfall now. It rains continuously with flooding from November to April. This is what is known as a bi-modal climate, typical of the warmer regions of the planet, six months intense rainfall and six months of drought. Ndola had 70 inches of rain in six months, the same as central Wales in twelve months. We kept the MGB for long runs on tar roads; its market value was 'peanuts'

Jo had developed a stomach ulcer. I took her to the new hospital in Ndola for a prescription for Aludrox SA. The Hungarian doctor was very pleasant. The scene at this new modern hospital was spoilt by the presence of a dead baby being lamented by the 14 year old mother and an angry father blaming the hospital and making political speeches. Someone said she had been feeding the baby on Coca Cola in response to the advertisement "Coke Adds Life".

11th December 1970

I removed my caravan, a Sprite Alpine, from Miengwe and had my government driver tow it to the Farmer Training Centre in Mpongwe. It was in a bad state internally after being used by the Swedes, which annoyed me somewhat. Jo and I followed in our new Peugeot 204 which went very well on the gravel road, 170 miles, via Miengwe, with comfortable suspension and very fast. It was small wonder that no one bought British cars in Africa anymore, they just fell to bits.

We walked all day in the sunshine with a local village headman named Kalola. We were getting to know the topography and soil indications. We found a deep lake in a fissure of limestone in an uninhabited area. Kalola said it was called *Inampamba* and he said it was connected underground with Kashiba Lake, "about a day's walk away". We thought his story about a cow getting drowned and coming up in Kashiba was less believable. Such gorgeous clear blue water and no fear of the dreaded bilharzia attracted us; we would be back with our swimming trunks.

"Kalola, are there any leopards around here?" I asked.

"No Mukwai. There used to be in my father's day but those miners have shot out everything and the skins are big money these days."

Vast areas of good land, such as this, in this rural district but with only a skeleton population, were a challenge for a land-use planner. Zambia had become so dependent upon maize from Rhodesia, and South Africa for goods and services, such that the only people thinking food were the few expatriate farmers in the south of the nation. It was so essential that these expatriate farmers were not frightened off by political extremists.

We later explored the 'dambo' or flood plain, behind our house in Itawa. We found interesting flora and birdlife, snipe in particular, a great challenge for shooters. I had brought my .22 calibre rifle with me on the plane with no questions asked. I always carried it in the 'bush'.

17th December 1970

Our two boys, Richard aged 18 and Philip, aged 15, arrived from England at last, by BOAC Super VC 10 in good spirits. Richard jumped into the M.G.B. with Philip as co-pilot and put his foot hard down for 20 miles to Luanshya to see Ann, the Mine Captain's daughter. They were feeling life was pretty good in Zambia. We all went to the Lowenthal Theatre to see '*A Christmas Carol*' with the Penningtons and Robert Taylor and June. An exciting Day One, followed by a sing-song with South African wine smuggled in.

The next day we took our boys on a 7 mile walk along Luanshya stream to see an enterprising small farmer who was responding to the call by KK to grow more food. I took Geoff White and my two Zambian deputies Tembo and Pongolati. Our boys were raised on the farm in Norfolk were keen to explore. So this African had made a pole barn to run tame rabbits and pigs. Rabbits were selling in Luanshya for two kwacha, £1, each, so with three litters per year of eight babies, he was making a bomb! We decided we would give this a go also, in our garden, using a Miengwe pig pen without a floor, running them loose on the soil and feeding them poultry pellets. They could dug holes in the lawn for nurseries.

Back in our office block Stephen Kaluwe our Zambian Chief Executive Officer was busy recruiting girls from secondary schools for the job of typist, one for me as well. I joined him. The girls were well spoken and of G.C.S.E. standard. It soon became apparent however, that Stephen's deciding factor was the contours of the girls' bottoms. He requested a twirl and his facial expressions, eyebrows particularly, gave the game away as to his final selection.

25th December 1970

Christmas was a very happy time for all of us, plus friends. Jo acquired a Beltsville White turkey from somewhere and Christmas Crackers too. The boys had brought gifts from the folks back home in the U.K. including Scrabble, a serious educational challenge for some! Boxing Day was a triumph. Two cars; the Peugeot via Luanshya to pick up Ann and the M.G. via the main tar road to the turning going west to Mpongwe and Inampamba Lake! Philip caught a nice bream for a campfire supper by the lake. We had the Sprite caravan now for overnight stops at the Farmer Training centre. The F.T.C. was run by a missionary vicar the Reverend Peter Bugg. Peter became a great friend over many years. Our new American Poultry Officer, Lester Grube joined us together with Geoff White and his wife. So Inampamba Lake, that had slumbered undisturbed for centuries, suddenly became a lido of scantily clad 'whites'.

The old village

Chief Nkambo's old village

The democratic planning process for Miengwe

Miengwe family farmer

Miengwe trial plot, maize

Self-built house with soil-cement blocks Miengwe

Miengwe 1, 2, and 3.

Miengwe 40, 50, 60.

k 500

SI𝒟𝒜 team leader.

Peter Borg

Our Sprite Alpine in Mpongwe with Philip, Rory, and Jo.

Inampamba bottomless Lake.

Off to Kitwe

CHAPTER FOUR

1971

1928 heralded all women in Britain as qualified to vote, hence as recently as the year I was born the U.K. became a true democracy. It had taken THAT long, after centuries of cruel wars, to achieve democracy, so it was hardly surprising that African nations recently 'liberated' from colonial rule should have problems in trying to establish true democracy. Uganda had suffered a military coup under Idi Amin. Here is a quote from The Times of Zambia in March 1971:- "A thin red line on the stonework of a remote bridge in Uganda marks the spot on which innocent young women and their boy-friends, army deserters, have been executed without trial and their bodies dropped to the fast-flowing waters of the Nile, infested with crocodiles, 70ft below. It is clear that President Amin's grip on the Government and the Army is not as strong as he would want the world to believe. Plagued by massive national debts, with consumer goods subject to 10% government sales tax, Amin is no better than Obote was. The basics here are tribal and internecine strife and an awful economy. There is really very little hope of the situation altering."

Decentralised government in Zambia 1979
Termite mounds are Zambia's soapbox

Zambia boys' army

Rice? "I don't think so"

The Biafran civil war in Nigeria had also been tragic. This had been tribal Ibo Christian south against tribal Muslim north. Rhodesia was now faced with war between black and white Rhodesians, a guerrilla war. A revolutionary war continued in Mozambique, communists backed by Chinese, versus the Portuguese. In Somalia strife was brewing between two sects of Muslims financed with ivory poached from Luangwa Valley, Zambia. In Sudan the Christian African south was in conflict with the Muslim Arab north. The Congo next door to Zambia was building for major war. In Angola strife continued, refugees were encamped in Western Zambia. So we were surrounded by warring nations. Were we safe? Jo and I had confidence in President Kenneth Kaunda, K.K., and his One Party State backed by wealth from efficiently mined copper. True democracy was working in Zambia and I was appointed a Returning Officer in Masaiti rural area!

21st January 1971

Affairs of the teenage hearts were coming to a head over the Christmas holiday. Mine Captain's daughter Ann had been staying with us in Ndola for five days. Richard and Ann enjoyed themselves bird watching in the extensive dambo behind the house, whilst Philip's mind was less upon binoculars and more upon my .22 rifle and the fat snipe in the swampy bits of the dambo. Luanshya mine cinema in the evenings had alternated with Scrabble, to test their vocabulary. The last film they saw, and possibly the most famous of the series, was *'Carry on Camping'*.

Alas, all too soon the day came for the boarding of the VC 10 for the U.K. Richard confided that "Ann had the wedding arrangement all worked out". What?! They were eighteen years old. The bountiful British Government was paying for their University and College education, but a married couple? We suspected that Mums and Dads might find that their financial responsibility had not quite terminated with their education. We missed the boys and we were faced with a postal strike in the U.K. which meant we would not receive news of their safe journey for some time.

Reflecting upon the adventurous freedoms in the open air enjoyed by the children in Zambia as opposed to the U.K.; the hunting instincts of boys, and the mothering instincts of the girls, seem to have become somewhat suppressed in modern times by the imperative of academic studies. Buying catapults or air rifles is suppressed in England and collecting birds' eggs and picking uncommon species of wild flowers is illegal. Are there so many country boys wanting to do that these days, as to pose a threat to conservation, as opposed to arousing an interest in 'natural history'? A devastating adverse impact on wildlife in UK did occur but it was not because of country boys robbing birds' nests, it was through joining the

EEC (EU). The CAP subsidy system made a chain of errors, one being payment for clearing over 25,000 miles of hedgerows to grow more corn, which became the 'grain-mountain'. It is so essential that children are enabled to enjoy touching wild things, like Nightjar eggs in Machiya

Our country boys

April 1971

With the rains easing up, we took off to explore the legendary Kashiba Lake seventy miles south of Ndola. We found a jewel in the landscape created by a huge calcite crystal oblong shape 'collapsed' in the vast limestone beds thus creating a sky blue lake with vertical walls much like an Olympic swimming pool. This special uniqueness was enhanced by the enclosing evergreen forest of uncommon species of trees and birds and the proclaimed bottomless depths of the lake. We noticed a bivouac nearby. Curiosity got the better of us and we found a young lady with 'a feller'. Oh! We recognised her from the women's ward at Ndola Hospital; a nursing sister.

We blew up our air bed and did some goggling, yes there were some fish, probably Bream. The Nurse told us "There are creepy stories about this lake and Africans say they never eat the fish from Kashiba because there are many dead people at the bottom and their spirits are pervasive guardians of the deep." The nurse repeated a story she had heard; "Six young warriors of the Kabena tribe captured a beautiful young girl of the local Mofya clan. They laid her across a limestone boulder and raped her, one after the other. She was ashamed and hurt. She could not return to her village pregnant as no-one would believe that she had not slept in another man's hut. So, in a state of deep depression, she drowned herself in Kashiba Lake. The family were not able to retrieve the body because the lake was so deep. The whole warrior class later died of poisoning by drinking the water, it was said. Many villagers of that tribe have drowned when fishing in the lake. It is an evil place, they say." Oh Dear!

Back in Ndola we discovered that my Zambian salary was long overdue and we were on an overdraft. Such was the additional hazard of working under the Overseas Service Aid Scheme where the Zambian Government pays me a standard African salary scale. The expatriate copper miners did not have that problem. Why did we do it? Well we opted for the post-colonial 'emerging nations' challenge and a bit of adventure, not forgetting a mind broadening experience for our children. My readers will gather that we were not 'on the Copperbelt' for the coppers. Madness, did you say? Bearing in mind our adventures in Tanzania, I would say "Africa is a priceless experience."

There was another reason why we were in Zambia when all the colonial public service employees were leaving; a psychological one perhaps: In the second phase of the Coventry Blitz in 1942 when I was age 13 yrs old, a high explosive bomb of German origin hit the kitchen outside door when I was standing two yards inside. The house fell down around me and I found myself standing upon the only clear spot looking up at the search lights in the sky. All the people next door were killed and I had a 'keepsake' in my arm but nothing worse. My father was away on Warden Duty and my mother under the stairs, so that the fact that I had survived Adolf's attempt to do away with me had left me, a good Christian Boy at the time, feeling that God had saved me for a reason. If he had thought that I was Missionary potential he certainly got that wrong. There was probably a psychological effect on me however and here I was, with the love of my life Jo, landed with the task of planning four agricultural projects under the Second National Development Plan of the Zambian Government.

Jo had to go for a DNC at the new Ndola Hospital. The building was impressive. Inside the shell, however, the old Northern Rhodesian African roots needed time. Jo went in at 7.30 am and found confidence with the female gynaecologist. Conditions in the new 'humanist' wards, however, were appalling and certainly not fit for ordinary humans with treatment reduced to 'bush' level. It was 'mealy meal' [maize meal], and water for all meals, and dozens of bed-less babies. Jo was shown respect by the few remaining skilled staff; however she was frightened and very sore when I collected her at 3.00 pm. The Doctor sent cancer test samples for Jo to the U.K. In view of the strike situation in England the results were not expected for at least a month.

We awaited news of our boys from the U.K. Apparently Ford Motor Company workers were also on strike for a 25% wage increase, the rail workers wanting a 15% increase and the Electricity Board likewise. It sounded like the death knell for British industry. Politicians thought that joining the European Economic Community was the solution. However, joining the Common Market required that you had something to sell at a competitive price. Communicating with the moon-walkers, Shepherd and Martin was easier than with our two boys in England.

All the animal kingdom have personal defence mechanisms, some of them quite extraordinary, but humans go one better, they have armies, not just for self defence but to kill the rest. The first thing each new 'independent' nation does is to create an army. Rumour had it that the Tanzanian Army was preparing to invade Uganda. A hooligan General Idi Armin had accomplished a *coup d'état* whilst the Kabaka, the elected President of Uganda, was away at the very civilised Commonwealth Conference in Singapore. President Nyerere was a dedicated supporter of democracy and supported the Kabaka. So it's Union Power in England and firepower in Africa.

More long tiresome meetings at Chapula Irrigation and Training Scheme near the city of Kitwe. Norman Beaumont, HQ Director of Rural Development, made his presence felt with a barrage of hard questions directed at the United Nations Manager, Jim Doyle. There were some very fine crops on show, irrigated by concrete water canals. The management was technically good but familiarity with the social problems of villager trainees, Chief Nkana's land rights, plot allocations, and so on, were difficult. Security for investors on traditional Chief's land is a brake on agricultural progress as it was in Saxon times in England. If I was to initiate major development in the vast fertile lands around Mpongwe in the south of the Province, I would have to persuade the Chiefs to relinquish their land to state ownership. It would take time to build that much trust in a white man.

Reflecting upon this revolutionary change in land tenure as occurred in Britain in 1066 AD; the Saxon concept was like the African pre-colonial one today where the resources for food production were provided by God, and the people were tenants under a Chief who allocated plots according to family size and tribal affiliation and not some national authority. The Normans divided land and water resources up between their Barons, under the King's control as conquerors, whom became landowners, thereby creating Freehold. Villagers were allocated plots for which they paid rent to the Lord of the Manor. They built themselves a cottage with a garden at their own expense and there was common land for their animals as in the New Forest today. Because of vested interests by landowners, the national economy prospered. In Zambia, development also depends upon a departure from the Saxon type of public tenure to State-owned land tenure, land being then sold or leased to private enterprise with guaranteed security. There was a complication however in 1971, unlike with William the Conqueror, the villagers had the Vote.

The Government of Zambia sent me a cheque for Kwacha 120 to keep me going. This was after some stern letters to the Ministry of Finance. Jo went shopping.

I conducted an official guest, a rice expert named Mr de Reau, across the Ndubeni/Kafue River flood plain. The water was three to four feet deep so we had to abandon the Land Rover and adopt a dug-out canoe. It is easy to capsize a roly-poly canoe so I took my .22 calibre rifle in case of crocodiles.

Jo was being left at home in Ndola rather too much, she said. Also, she said, we needed to socialise with our neighbours. The Falconer family opposite had three young children whom played in our garden a lot but they had no school. This gave Jo the idea of using her teaching skills from her years employed by the Norfolk Education Committee and she planned for a small school in our large house for European and South African children, to prepare them for their entrance exams to Secondary boarding schools overseas. She would be able to use the P.N.E.U. correspondence course used by Diplomats on Overseas Assignments. P.N.E.U. stands for Parents National Education Union. She would be able to charge a fee which would resolve our current solvency problems. We'd have to use our house as a private school.

Jo had a natural affinity with children in terms of classroom discipline. She was very strict, giving the children confidence which made them love her because of her kind nature and underlying good humour. This doubtless arose from her mother Eva Marriott (nee Eva Durrant) who married late after a career as a trained nanny before World War I at Great Ormond Street Children's Hospital. She became Nanny to Sir Peter Scott when his father was in the disastrous Antarctic Expedition and later to Lord Killearn and Lady Lampson. Lord Killearn was the British Ambassador in Japan at the time, followed by China and later Cairo during WWI. Eva was a mine of knowledge upon handling children.

The London Times newspaper reported 20% of eleven year olds could barely write. We should not have that problem in Ndola schools. **Times of Zambia:** "The M.P. for Ndola claims that 'expatriate teachers are afraid of disciplining their pupils. I do not know why. Zambia is going backwards as far as education is concerned. Today's students are rude and could not be called educated. Teachers, especially expatriates, are equally guilty of rudeness. Some of them, like their pupils, even have lice in their hair.' he said."

We had news from the U.K.at last. The postal strike was to end after seven weeks, 25 million letters awaited clearance. Ford Motor Company had lost £25 million.

I joined the Photographic Club and set up a dark room for black and white portrait photography. So, many beautiful ladies appeared in my dark room henceforth, as I am sure they will remember to this day!

Jo was brought two baby owls by a member of the Conservation Society. They were all fluff, huge eyes and prominent beaks. They would capture your attention by staring with big black eyes and hissing. Jo tried a sloppy mixture of bread and milk on a spoon; snap, claws, spitting. Jo withdrew her hand, dripping with blood. We sat and stared at each other while they hissed their displeasure at being in our company. Jo suggested trying a squeegee soap bottle. A squirt to the back of the throat when the beak opened started a route to the future. The smallest owl was less clever and got covered beak to tail in milk and egg, needing a bath. The next day, a friend brought us a pair of industrial gloves which made the whole process a lot easier. We named the biggest one Twoo and the little one Twit. We decided Twit and Twoo needed meat, hence chicken livers from a friend, Mrs O'Dell who farmed out of town. We darned them with wool and covered the meat with their own down from their cage. Every other day we gave them cotton wool. They began producing pellets.

Twit and twoo

After a couple of weeks, we were all accommodated and they grew rapidly. Twoo became a very handsome bird but both remained spiteful and mistrustful. Then one day when Jo was cleaning their cage they escaped and flew away into the distance, far away over Itawa dambo, never to be seen again. We felt sad and a hug was called for. Our relationships with the wild were always fleeting.

"Keeping animals and birds in cages, reminds me Brian, of when **we** were trapped in the severe restrictions of war-time, as teenagers. When you and I met at a dance in the Village Hut, it was love at first sight wasn't it; "two lovely people" everyone said, and away we flew, like Twit and Twoo, to Africa."

Kashiba Weekend

There are gnomes with long red noses, goblins, ogres and *imfwiti* lurking in the forests of the Lamba speaking people. They certainly exist in the minds of every Lamba man, woman and child, no matter what may be their standard of education. Lamba teenage boys and girls do not sneak off into the forest for sex; they are made aware that the *imfwiti* which leap along the forest paths at night may catch them. *Imfwiti* are adapted for leaping along narrow pathways at speed between the tress, being human-like but with only one leg. They have glowing eyes like owls and hands with claw-like nails for preventing their victim's escape. We decided that we would chance it and camp by this heavenly beautiful lake in the forest.

We knew Chieftainess Ndubeni of the local clan of this superstitious tribe, called Akashiba Kabena. We were glad of the shade of her sitting room, the clay brick walls decorated with Catholic pictures from St Anthony's Italian Mission, reminding callers where the truth lay and the threat to disbelievers posed by the devil. This elderly dignified lady was dressed in patriotic loose cottons, emblazoned with UNIP Party Leaders portraits and slogans, her head wrapped in a turban. She smoked continuously and coughed between sentences and warned Jo and I about camping near the lake. We enquired over a cup of weak, sickly sweet tea, traditionally served to honoured guests, why it was that local Africans never went near the lake, even to draw water or to fish?

Chieftainess Ndubeni

Kashiba Lake

Richard and Philip dicing with death in Kashiba Lake.

"You must not drink that water, nor eat the fish, nor indeed immerse your bodies in the water as you white people like to do, for beneath the waves lies the spirits of the extinct Mofya clan." I asked sceptically how that could be. She sat upright in her lounging chair, a small lean figure and clasping the good luck charm suspended from her neck, she explained with a stern face the "The Mofya, or goat clan, were greatly oppressed by the superior clan, the Kabena, who frequently stole their goats and raped their women. The Kabena also boasted that they washed their hands in human blood. The Mofya people became quite obsessed with their inability to repel the Kabena and finally determined to commit mass suicide. They all tied themselves together in a line and jumped into the bottomless depths of Kashiba Lake."

She finally ended her tale with a smile. "There is a twist in the tale of this story as they say. The last girl at the end of the line had a lover of the Kabena clan who was hiding in the bushes nearby until her turn came, when he jumped out and with his sword, he cut the rope. When the Italian missionaries came and built St Anthony's Mission, the lovers adopted the Catholic faith and founded a strong clan of people. Those two lovers are the ancestors of all people that live in the villages by the lake today. But they know that the Goat Clan spirits are always ready to draw them to the bottom of the lake if they swim in it. So they keep well away, as you must also do!"

I thanked her politely for her advice and Jo and I took our leave, fully intending to demonstrate the superiority of the white man's spiritual influence. Such a glorious azure blue heaven for bathers could not be resisted. This rectangular lake was seemingly bottomless by dint of the fact that it nestled in a collapsed limestone cavity. As we set up our tent, the silence unnerved us for a while and we found ourselves speaking in whispers. The surrounding Dry Evergreen Forest loomed over our camp shading us from the sun.

The temperature was soaring and we couldn't wait any longer to immerse ourselves in Kashiba's still, cool water. One could barely see the surface exactly as it so matched the sky. We noticed the cooing of the rare *Narina trogon,* and spotted it perched bolt upright amongst the evergreens, swelling its crimson breast and fluffing its bright green wings. We decided that it was a hallmark of the lake, a guardian in the shade, cooing like a dove over its 'charges', those tragic watery spirits. We felt reluctant to disturb the trogon or its 'charges' at the bottom of the lake. However, after a while the blue water became irresistible and we stripped off, and holding hands we jumped naked into the silent blue water. As we hit the water and rose up to speak, we found ourselves talking in whispers again echoing, rather like being in a cathedral. We swam out a little, feeling our way over the bottomless depths. An eerie feeling came over us, like free-falling. Jo wanted to get out, she said that she had a feeling that she was being dragged down.

At that moment, she disappeared and I plunged down after her in great alarm. I spotted her hair floating wildly below me, already six feet down. I am not that good a swimmer. In a panic, I mustered adrenaline and plunged down some more. The tips of my fingers touched her hair and twizzling it as hard as I could I managed to begin lifting by kicking upwards. It was heavy going and I had to kick harder and harder. My breath was about finished when I hit the surface and took a gasp, plunging down again to help her up. She was exhausted and I had to swim back with her on her back, dragging her. Needless to say we didn't swim again, we sat on the rocks above, trembling and drying off, shocked and tense.

Skinny Dipping
The thrill of African skinny dipping is more than just the joy of cool water on hot naked skin. You have to visualise the absence of people in remote locations, like the dams I built on Mufulira Ranch, Inampamba Lake and volcano crater lakes, such as Ngualla and Masoko in Tanzania, and the intense blue sky, no aeroplanes, absolute silence, or maybe the chortling cry of a fish eagle. However one needed to be aware that such temptations had their risks such as wild buffalo in hundreds coming down to join you when the sun sank, or bilharzia, or snakes on shallow shore lines; no

paramedics if you sank too deep or are attacked by monsters of the deep in Kashiba Lake. Kashiba was a wild and silent place. The walls were vertical and high so that the only way in as to dive. Getting out was quite difficult.

"Brian, there is something black moving in the bushes over there, look!"

"They are scuba divers; from the mine I expect. Let's walk around and warn them."

The conversation went something like this: "Hello there, are you going down then?"

"Yes, we have heard this story about human remains in the bottom so we thought we would go down and take a look to settle the matter for good and all. We should be able to see in this clear water. It depends how deep it is though."

"Do you come from the Copperbelt?"

"Yes, Mufulira."

"I work around here as a Land Surveyor" I told them. "I have plumbed the depth of Kashiba; I dropped four 100 ft survey chains to touch the bottom 396 feet. That was at the edge."

"Good God! Well, we are used to deep shafts in the mines. It might be dark that far down though, I am not sure. We'll give it a go. I'll go half way and watch over John as he goes deeper."

"Do you think we will ever see them again Jo? Maybe they'll just add to the pile already down there!"

Suddenly there was a swirl and the man surfaced, shouting excitedly.

"Something has happened to John! I am going down to look for him. Can you please go up to the Mission for help?"

"OK I'll send Jo. Good luck!"

It seemed a long while before the surface broke again. Two Italian priests arrived with blankets. A floating body appeared and then the other man began struggling with him to the rock wall. It was a major struggle to get the body out.

"He's alive; I think. I managed to get the air pipe into his throat. His visor is smashed."

We took turns 'pumping him out' and how relieved we were when he coughed. Up at the mission later, the injured man recovered enough to tell us what happened.

"I descended rapidly, almost as though I was being sucked down, I have never had such a falling feeling in water. Keeping the white wall in sight and my colleague above me in the bright light, I reached about 300 ft. My suit was pressing hard about me and the light was weak, but I could make out a cave and went over to investigate. There was a human skeleton draped over the ledge which I was peering down at, when I became aware

71

of a presence. Glancing up, there were shiny 'piggy' eyes approaching from within the cave. A large face gradually grew up around the unblinking eyes, grey, with a trailing beard and arms below just like an old man. Suddenly he hit me with something and then swung around and came at me again like a torpedo striking me with a head butt in the face. The glass in my diving mask broke and I lost vision. I had the presence of mind to release my weighted belt before clasping my diving mask to reduce air loss. I couldn't see the old man any more. I panicked and took in water and I must have lost consciousness because I don't remember Jim rescuing me, but I tell you what, there is a ghost of those dead people down there and it's no puff of smoke, it's a monster!"

Much later on, I read a report on Kashiba Lake questioning the wisdom of encouraging tourists to swim in the lake. Neiles Billany, who was a North Sea oil-rig diver at the time of writing, was born in Mufulira in the Copperbelt descending from a copper mining father and grew up to be a scuba diver in Zambia. "I would not dive to the bottom of Kashiba, not even with my North Sea equipment. Maybe the water spirit was kind to us all those years ago but I would be more respectful today."

In Africa, stock theft gets harsher punishment than manslaughter. This is the clip from the Times of Zambia of 18th June 1971: "Harry Saidi, 30 of Sabena Burns Township and Richard Banda, 34, of Washeri Township, Kitwe, were sentenced in Ndola Crown to seven years hard labour each for killing one goat and one sheep worth Kwacha 50 and stealing the animals from the farm of Mr Peter Steynberg on 30th December 1970. They were also ordered to get ten strokes each. Both pleaded guilty to stock theft."

I had heard of poachers being arrested by government Wildlife Rangers, probably local people finding meat for the Chief's pot. This was in Senior Chief Machiya's area in the far south west corner of the Province bounded by the mighty Kafue River. Chief Machiya confirmed that government Rangers had been there but local villagers refused to co-operate with them so that they failed to apprehend any poachers from the mining towns. "Hmmm, I thought, *this system of central Game Department harassing villagers is doomed to failure. I need a plan. Call it Game Management Area No. 23.*

I drove along the rough bush track in Machiya that the fishermen used to get to the prolific Luswishi River from which they caught fish to be sold in Luanshya. They were there in their pick-up truck early in the mornings. The men spoke English and told me a tale about one of their friends who encountered a lion. His name was Andrew Sakala and he was with his uncle near the river when he heard a rustling in the tall grass. "A Puku antelope leapt out across my path and I sighed with relief. I said, we'll bring the gun next time we come. Meat fetches a good price in Ndola."

Andrew asked the old man to tell us about the scar on his leg. "I shot six lions and then I was careless. I shot one but didn't kill it. It is bad to leave a lion like that; it'll go mad and kill the villagers. I reloaded my gun and went into the long grass following the trail of blood. It was a powerful male. The skin was just right for the floor of a miner's house and worth good money. I followed it a long way and it was getting dark when I saw it but not before it saw me. It was a good shot and killed it before it landed on top of me. Its body was still racing and his claws gashed my leg really badly. All night I lay under the lion until villagers came for fishing in the morning. They took me to Mpongwe Mission but the wound was festering."

The story teller said that the man swore he would never let a lion come near him or his village again and "so many lions were killed which was good because the Puku antelope increased and gave them food. The lion skins gave the miners a chance to pretend to their friends that they were courageous lion hunters."

CHAPTER FIVE

1972

January 1972 – Food Shortages

Our boys had been home with us for Christmas. We now had our own rabbit production unit in the garden, 27 rabbits all told. This was a rustic pig pen from Miengwe V.R. Scheme, without a floor so they dug holes for nurseries; free-for-all sex was the order of the day. I left a note for Richard as Jo and I left early for the 40 mile drive to Miengwe Settlement Scheme:

1. Tell John to wash the MGB before you drive to Luanshya to pick up Ann.
2. Check the rabbits. If there is a feral cat in the pen, get the .22 rifle out.
3. Check with Peter what happened to the seed potatoes! The seed bed is ready for Philip to demonstrate his gardening skills!
4. I will get some money from the bank tomorrow to stimulate progress.

Our son Richard, from his year dot had been a farmer's boy, having all the skills related to producing food and loving the farm animals and the wildlife of the English countryside. Living in Africa had cultivated his love of nature. Now a young adult, he cared about the welfare of people as well as animals. His chance of becoming a farmer in UK, however, was nil, since the only way in was inheritance. So his destiny had to be between food processing or caring for people and animals. Ann was training to be a teacher, and loved cats, they should get on.

Caroline was now married and living in Japan, aged 22 years old, travelling the world with her shipping agent husband. Philip was six years younger than Caroline, a different character, destined to go his own way as an adventurer, a risk taker. He wanted to be a Wildlife Ranger in Africa. Philip had his eye on Nancy Wagstaff's daughter Susan and wanted to take her off to explore the wilds of Zambia's National Parks in due course "confronting danger together", he said.

We loaded our boys once more onto the VC10 for England and stepped-back into sad reflection; *what's going on here? It wasn't supposed to be like this.*

Jo and I were now only 43 years old and faced with finding a whole new purpose in life, new bonding activities, in the face of our children fledging the nest. We became soul-mates in our teenage years and had pursued the same ambitions all our lives, but we hadn't contemplating an early ending; were we equipped for a whole new life together? Our WWII upbringing did have a bearing upon our understanding of sincerity in personal relationships; oath taking was serious stuff during the war. Fortunately our oxytocin levels were as high as ever, rising in fact.

And so began our dancing years in Ndola. So many clubs for Saturday evening rave-ups in addition to the Savoy Hotel which had a fabulous Congolese band keeping everyone on the floor. This ecstasy episode of wild joy on the dance floor was terminated one evening when our friend Ann du Bruhn discovered that the hotel manager was a German. She was, like us, a veteran of WWII. There he was on the balcony overlooking the dancers. Ann became flushed, her eyes staring with hatred, she stood up, seemingly petrified. She suddenly raced up the stairs shouting in Dutch. She slapped the manager's face and attempted to push him over the balcony rail only to be restrained by her husband Tom from committing murder. There was a heated exchange of swearwords in Dutch and German. The Band fell silent in wonderment at such female fury and we had to take refuge in my car en route for some Camomile tea at our house. Tom explained how it came about that the lovely Ann had been raped during the war by a German Officer during a rebellious confrontation with the Gestapo.

Britain in the 1970's was in a state of economic and political collapse, many people emigrated, the housing market fell into the doldrums, British cars became unsalable in the Commonwealth of fifty four nations, unlike in the colonial times when British cars were a post war miracle, such as the E type Jaguar, the Morris Minor and of course the Land Rover. Yet, in this decade of despair popular music became a worldwide triumph of creativity, still played regularly today 47 years later. Pop groups that spring joyfully to my mind; Abba in 1974, The Osmonds, Queen, The Three Degrees, Tobacco Road, David Bowie, Hot Chocolate, Daddy Cool from the West Indies, The Beatles, T.Rex *Get it on*, B J Thomas, from the USA, Stevie Wonder and The Bee Gees. The Rolling Stones, Status Quo, Tom Jones The Equals, The Kinks, Rod Stewart and our beloved Kenya songster Roger Whitaker. We even had a jazz band in Itawa regularly rehearsing in our sitting room with Lester Grube, our American Poultry Officer, on the drums. Every Saturday we were out dancing at one of the many clubs in Ndola, a different club each week, meeting different groups of people – none of them agricultural of course, because Ndola was a hub of industry.

Jazz at home

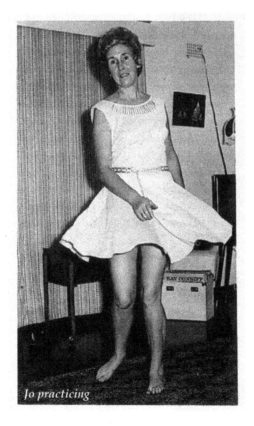

Jo practicing

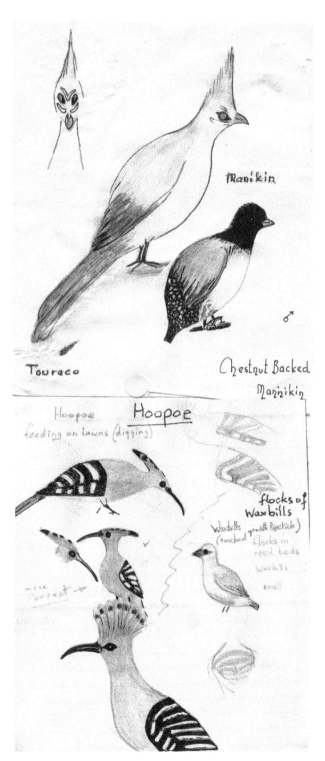

Manikin

Toureco

Chestnut Backed
Mannikin

♂

Hoopoe
feeding on lawns (digging)

Hoopoe

flocks of
Waxbills

Waxbills (youth with lipstick)
(touched) flocks in
reed beds
Waxbills
small

more
correct →

We joined the Bird Group of the Wildlife Conservation Society of Zambia, which took us out into 'the bush' with binoculars. I was good at drawing, as a map maker, and my diary became loaded with pictures of colourful birds. My growing fascination with birds extended to the dance floor, enjoying colourful attire, lyrical rhythms, intrigue, and excitement. For a forty four year old male, the potential for flirting rather than 'flighting' called for some restraint.

Two new Swedish Volunteers arrived at Miengwe, though strictly speaking, they were not Swedish; Giri Novak was a refugee from Communist Czechoslovakia who escaped with a pocketful of diamonds given to him by his grandmother so that he was able to buy a car. Johan Slotte was from Finland, hence his knowledge of the original Sauna, which he duly constructed behind the Swedish house at Miengwe, fuelled by wood. The Miengwe sauna became notorious with the Swedish community of Ndola, a rallying point for Jo and Brian also. The Swedish often expressed the view that the Brits were an idle lot of layabouts, largely true in the U.K. at that time. This was assuaged by our good relations in the sauna plus cold beer and all stark naked in Finnish style. Sauna is pronounced sowna. There was no thought of admiring the opposite sex - get into the cold shower or die. We had our caravan to retreat to. I have to say that the experience was quite the most exciting exercise that the human body can endure, Finnish style that is. However, one needs to be fit to survive it in the tropics. Norman Beaumont, my boss and a lot older than me, declined because he feared a heart attack.

Ann and Tom du Bruhn loved our expeditions into the wilds of Machiya where I was formulating an anti-poaching scheme based upon local initiative instead of central government control. Robert Taylor came too, as usual, and photographed us wading through the swamps. We camped out for the week-end, by the Luswishi River, absolutely teeming with small fish. It was a wild place, Puku antelope everywhere on the flood plain.

Machiya swamps

Rifle at the ready.　　Courtesy Ann du Bruhn

Game Management Area No. 23

My proposal was to select local men approved by Chief Machiya and the District Council and send them for training by the Government Game Department. After I had formally presented this idea to a University gathering of conservationists and government officials in Lusaka there was formal applause but much disbelief that they could trust a local Chief and village headmen not to exploit their legal authority to do a bit of game cropping themselves. My idea was to build responsibility at local council level by requiring them to pay the Game Guards wages. The local governance would then have a vested interest in driving out poachers and collecting hefty licence fees from selected legitimate hunters which could be used to build a school and a road.

The Game Department eventually agreed and sent a Piper Cub plane, donated by W.W.F. to fly me around the area and do a game count at low level. I could not take Jo because there was no insurance with government planes. After a three hour delay at take-off from Ndola airport, I later realised that a full bladder was inappropriate to the task in hand, especially when flying low over the vast Lukanga Swamps en route. In desperation I implored the pilot to land at Mpongwe Mission. He declared that he was not permitted to do that. Panic stations! I noticed the flight chart behind the seat was enclosed in a thick flexible plastic envelope. Unfortunately it was designed with exposed corners. I hurriedly removed my shoe-laces and, ever resourceful, tied up the corners. After removal of the chart, a substantial balloon of urine enabled me to concentrate on counting the Puku.

Our interest in the wild-side of Ndola was growing; that is to say, 'clubbing'. Jo dressed up in her orange sackcloth material dress with a side thigh split and diamond studded stockings. We loved the Rugby Club Tramps Ball. The music was by Liquid Island, which kept us going until 3.00 am. At 8.30 am we had a date with the Bird Watcher Group. Jo could hardly walk for stiff legs.

Great Day for Jo and Brian

Two army helicopters arrived fifty minutes early. I had not had a chance to put a film in my camera. I had a guest at Miengwe, His Excellency Dr Kenneth Kaunda, President of Zambia no less. The anthill beckoned, the famous white handkerchief came out, emotional words, and much cheering. Jo and I had K.K. to ourselves without any security interference as we visited settled family farmers who joyfully showed him their new houses. Next came the crop-trial plots. K.K. asked Jo, resplendent in her borrowed English straw bonnet, to show him around the Rural Health Centre. This was not the plan, because the Minister of Health was present. Our Swedish Volunteers demonstrated their brick making machine, with which his Excellency was hugely impressed and congratulated the Volunteers warmly, whereupon they showed him and his whole Cabinet around their Swedish thatched roof house. Peter Borg's guitar which was hanging on the wall caught the eye of the President. He requested to try it and he proved well able to play it happily. Jo took a photo of this distinguished group in front of the house for posterity.

K.K. expressed a wish to address the settlers again before departure, whereupon he congratulated them for their courage and enterprise and invited more to join the Scheme. The Provincial Cabinet Minister provided his car for K.K. to be driven to Mpongwe to address the people of the Copperbelt Rural District from the Mission Hospital. He invited Jo and I to accompany him in his car; with no security. Good humoured chat with a white English lady and the Provincial Land-use Planning Officer to whom he expressed his desire for me to provide him with a write-up of the "Miengwe Formula" as he put it. Volunteer Jiri Novak and his girlfriend Bo Fredlund, followed us to Mpongwe in his new little Fiat car and was able to transport us back home to Ndola in time to watch a film of the day's events on T.V. We had been so impressed with President Kaunda's humility, politeness and dignity. He was truly the Father of the Nation.

June 1972.

Soon after this event, Caroline arrived from Japan, hoping to meet her brothers shortly in their summer recess from England. She was rather thin after food poisoning on the plane from India and wore a deep frown. We were determined to restore her happy laughing persona. Philip had been awarded; school Sportsman of the Year and the Victor Ludorum Trophy from the Warwickshire County Council. Our two boys were now home. More and more rabbits kept popping up from the tunnels in our 'floorless' garden summer house. It was a most pleasing aspect of communism.

My 'Mienglae' guest
H. President Kaunda

D. Chintibe   B. Dewhy -Bulawayo   K Kaunda

Brian's friend

We marshalled friends Jo and Brian Falconer and Maureen and Brian Mottram, both accountants for the mining company headquarters Roan Consolidated Mines. It was time to hit the 'bush', in other words Wild Africa, which for Jo and Brian Falconer was a new experience. We set off for Inampamba Lake. The lake lay 4.5 miles off the gravel road into the deserted landscape of limestone boulders and scrub. This exciting spot was unknown to the vast urban community of the Copperbelt. However, having said that, we encountered a tent housing a couple; Duncan and his wife Maggie who had a laughing baby of four months with them. What kinds of people endure these primitive conditions? Well the answer is, geologists in Africa do. Duncan was Canadian but born in Kenya and Margaret was from Los Angeles. We invited them to Ndola with their laughing baby for the weekend break.

Inampamba Lake.

Week end
Alan and Betty
Dunsmuir

The water was clear and blue; we could see fish, temptingly. Other temptations for the three Brian's especially were how little cladding the two Jo's could get away with when basking in the tropical sun under a blue heaven. Jo Falconer was the acknowledged expert in diverting Brian's eye away from the feathered variety.

"Jo, there's fresh elephant droppings behind that rock you're lying on, can't you smell it? They come here to drink, at about 4 o'clock."

"Brian! – Falconer, "What time is it?"

"Time for you to put the kettle on Jo!"

My studies of tropical soil science had taught me that African continental soils are senile and of very low fertility as compared to soils in the temperate regions of the planet. The best tropical soils are dark red, as per Miengwe, which were always sought after by the missionaries for their stations. Yet even these red clays have very poor 'cation exchange' capacity which means they do not retain the essential elements from fertiliser for long, and are, oddly enough, free draining; imagine that, no sticky clay in Africa. As a result chemical fertilisers will feed maize only for a limited period. However on those vast limestone beds surrounding Inamapamba Lake the soils are very productive. So why are they unused for cropping? I will explain later and just enjoy the swimming in 'safe water'.

One might suppose that this poverty in the soil mantle might extend to the flora and fauna, but No. There are more species of animal and vegetable in Africa than anywhere else on the Planet, with Amazonia a close second. However, abundant avian species do need to fly north, annually for survival, as did the early human spp. apparently. So what do we conclude from this discourse by the "absent-minded Professor", as Nancy Wagstaff always called me. The white folks love tropical holidays, but our health, wealth and prosperity depends upon the climate and fertile soils of the temperate zones.

Philip apparently broke all the rackets at the squash club in Ndola. He was now tall in a family of very small people on both sides. The DNA for gigantism seems to lurk in the shadows of all families, yet we are told by archaeologists that our Serengeti ancestors, *Homo habilis,* were only four feet tall. The Japanese and the primitive Bushmen tribe of the Botswana desert are uniformly only five feet. It must be something to do with finding food. Philip had an enormous appetite and was going to need a good cook as a wife. Sue Wagstaff filled the bill. They were planning a safari to Luangwa National Park together later that year.

The Times of Zambia detailed the financial misfortunes of the nation; copper price was at record lows at around £1,435 per ton. This compares with the 2017 current price of £4,500 per ton. Zambia had only two commodities for export, copper and tobacco. Copper, £280 million and tobacco £24 million, with imports stated to be £350 million from the U.K. and £35 million from Europe. This, therefore, was my problem with the lack of funds for projects like Miengwe, and for my salary being late.

BIG NEW PLAN TO BOOST FOOD SUPPLIES.
The route to developing this Mpongwe area was illustrated here: The Times of Zambia headline on 27th July 1972. "THE PLAN" This was recognition of my proposal for the Chiefs to relinquish their land, amounting to almost half of the Copperbelt Province, to the Government, hence to become State Land with legal freehold tenure for sale to investment companies to grow food. It remained for me to survey the boundary, prepare a reconnaissance soil map and publish. It had taken me four years to gain the Chiefs' confidence to agree to this. The Minister of Rural Development Mr Kamanga reviewed the plan in an exclusive interview to Business Review:

"The Ministry of Rural Development is to launch a massive multi-crop irrigation scheme in the Kafue Basin in Ndola Rural in a bid to reduce Zambia's dependence upon imported foodstuffs. Wheat, barley, potatoes and potato seed, beans, sugar cane and other vegetables are to be grown on a large scale in the Munkumpu irrigation pilot scheme in the Mpongwe

area south of Luanshya, covering 20,000 hectares of virgin land. " NB. There was a bit of confusion here; Munkumpu was the trial plots for all those crops (plus bananas) whilst the major irrigation scheme plan for wheat and soya beans covered 20.000 hectares.

I had flown with the Minister Reuben Kamanga over the whole Mpongwe area and I found him a very sociable, educated gentleman. He had achieved some German Aid for research in Munkumpu, Ndubeni, and I soon enjoyed a team of soil surveyors wearing grey World War Two army serge suits and hats. Their smartly dressed manager spoke in impeccable English. We entertained him to dinner in our lovely house in Ndola. Guess what? Rabbit stew! This resulted in us being invited to Germany on our next leave. Since their prodigy Adolf did his utmost to kill me in 1942, not to mention my Uncle Tom in the Libyan Desert, I was not enamoured with the idea of us spending our leave there.

A Dutch man, Dr Peter Heilmann, was posted to my team of soil surveyors for the Mpongwe Development Zone. Peter's wife Yoke had two children Peter and Mariska, would soon attend Jo's school to upgrade their English. We set up a pilot crop trials area in Munkumpu, to be managed by Mt Makulu Research Station of Lusaka, to trial bananas, wheat, soya beans and citrus fruit crops. This sub-research station was later sold to Colonial Development Corporation for £3 million. The Ndola Rural District Council never dreamt that they could ever carry such a huge sum of money in their Treasury.

September 1972 Lake Malawi.
Philip had gone back to school and we were preparing for a wedding in December. Ann talked about having her 'hen-night' on Lake Malawi, how exotic was that idea. It was a heck of a long drive in the Peugeot 204. I was shattered. Dr David Livingstone put me to shame however, as he walked from Nyasaland to Victoria falls at the age of 40 in 1852. One wonders what he ate en route. It certainly wasn't cans of Heinz Baked Beans that's for sure! We were served excellent food at the Grand Beach Hotel on the lake shore. Richard jumped into a solo dinghy and went off sailing as per his Tanga days in Tanzania. I climbed the hill with Jo and sat wondering at the works of nature, the vastness of blue water like an inland sea, is 11,248 sq miles in extent and deeper than the sea level, they say at 2,316 ft, the third deepest lake in the world. Lake Victoria is very shallow by comparison at 270 ft. In fact Lake Malawi lies in one of the African Rift Valleys.

The mighty Lake Malawi

There's a lot of fish in Lake Malawi - Was.

We sat on granite hills from two and half billion years ago, sensing the lake shoreline populated with fishermen's villages with smoking straw roofs, and everywhere flocks of colourful birds; an ornithologist's paradise. I just had to draw them in my diary. For Jo and I to sit and relax with no itinerary of work and travel for me, was uncomfortable. We didn't fit in with the lazy casualness of lakeside sun and dreaming. Everybody else loved it here including our friends the Van de Polls from Lusaka whom we co-ordinated the holiday with. I found some garnets on the beach; the sand was quite red in places.

The next day Vil. [Wihelm] Van de Poll suggested she and I climbed the hill together whilst Jo was socialising with the children on the beach. I liked Vil. very much and we sat together in the silent wildness for a long time talking about life in Africa and what motivated us. We had both become sceptical about religion and the 'evils' committed by the many missionaries in Africa by destroying native culture. We had both been Christian devotees in our youth. We were getting into emotional deep water after a couple of hours. I muttered something about it being 'sundowners' time and we descended the slopes hand in hand to find Jo looking a bit 'straight faced'.

We all loved the sailing but not much wind for fun and games. Richard and Ann were getting to know each other intimately. Courting on a beach in Malawi had to be romantic for two twenty year olds. There was a full moon over the lake on the 19th September, heralding the start of a new episode, which indeed proved to be the case for Richard and Ann. They sailed out to a granite island named Namalenje about two miles off shore which they had seen glowing white in the moonlight. It proved to be guano from a population of two species of White Necked Cormorants. They must have inhabited it for centuries. There was a Monitor Lizard population there too, doubtless enjoying a chicken and egg diet.

26th September 1972
We left Malawi and headed for Chipata town in Zambia at 9.00 am. We met Ben Van de Poll there with the road blocked by hundreds of youths in green uniforms, marching amidst cheering crowds. They were National Service recruits. Most new African nations had compulsory National Service. Later we were deviated down some very rough tracks because of a road accident. We discovered an overturned army lorry with one dead body. The locals had no idea how to clear the road so we all piled in to help the few militia there. Richard took a photo; fatal mistake – he was apprehended and accused of being a spy. Jo became angry, as was her nature – "no-one messes with Jo Dawtrey" – and began assaulting one of the soldiers. They swore at her very rudely. Richard took the film cassette out of his camera and handed it over, which permitted us to depart. We

worried a lot about what would be the outcome when they developed the film.

When the time came for Ann and Tom de Bruhn to leave Zambia they left their beloved Dachshund with us. Unfortunately when Richard was setting off for Luanshya in the MGB   to see his fiancé Bartji's lead caught in the door with him outside the car, so that Bartji had to run like hell for quite some distance before Richard stopped thinking he had a tyre problem. So Bartji began life with Jo and Brian, with four very sore pads, and Richard with rather a lot of explaining to do to regain his mother's admiration. Bartji became a very ferocious guard dog where Africans were concerned, but immensely loving with Jo – it was quite a love affair. Intelligent Bartji was with us for two fearless years, driving intruders away from our rabbits. We now had two geese and two Muscovy ducks also, but they were quite aggressive and kept me, and Bartji, at bay, sadly not so one day, years hence, the security guard from next door made the mistake of fancying a goose for supper and was apprehended by the ankle. He had big hob-nail boots on and kicked Bartji to death. Our black/white relationship was put to the test.

30th December 1972

30th December 1972

My diary states, "Acquired another daughter." A brief statement of fact belied a glorious white wedding with bridesmaids at the Church in Luanshya followed by a tumultuous reception at Makoma Yacht Club with so many good friends; many of whom have kept in touch with us all for the rest of our lives.

At the time of writing; the happy couple have now been together for forty five years. They spent their honeymoon in our caravan before returning to England to find employment, aged twenty years old. They were not, as adults, permitted to remain in Zambia without a Work Permit. They vaguely hoped that they might receive some help "as refugees" to settle in England, arriving as they did at the same time as the 24,000 Asians refugees from Uganda, expelled by Idi Amin. However it was not to be, "you stand on your own feet if you're born British."

Richard and Ann's Luanshya wedding.
1972

Sister Caroline, father and mother

Who made this magnificent cake?

All one family now.

Baluba Mine Captain Jack Hartley, R., Ann, Jo, Philip.

CHAPTER SIX

1973

In January 1973
Our daughter Caroline, over from Mombasa for the wedding of her brother Richard to Ann, stayed on for January. We were overjoyed to be a family altogether again probably for the last time in Africa. I took her to see my project in Miengwe. Caroline was born and raised on a Norfolk farm, hence genuinely interested in the way the Lamba villagers were building themselves houses and keeping small pig and poultry units. The village headmen told her how happy they were with tap water, a school and a Health Centre with a government medical assistant. It looked like real progress, at the grass-roots.

Caroline expressed her understanding of the reason why we were doing this but; "Dad, I am concerned for you and Mum's safety, you being the only white person around in the rural area, employed by the government, in a nation of so called freedom fighters who have just escaped from the clutches of a white racist regime."

"Your mum and I are treated with the utmost respect by the hierarchy here; well, except for a bit of a fracas with the Senior Chief Mushili that got into the national press. I had the heavies on my side though and the Chief eventually accepted me as an ally rather than a threat to his authority. The other Chiefs think I am a useful chap to have around; Senior Chief Machiya is enjoying a puku antelope roast at weekends without being prosecuted; Chief Nkana's people have got irrigated vegetable plots earning them good money in Kitwe City market; Chieftainess Ndubeni has a government crop trials plot keeping her in corn, bananas and avocados. Oh yes, Chief Malembeka in the South, will soon have bore-holed water for his people as a result of tobacco growing scheme. So they know that I am not here to exploit them, as has been their experience in the past."

"Dad, this is an unstable country under threat from Ian Smith in Rhodesia who has closed the border and has an army patrolling the Zambezi River. The Zambian army just shot two young Canadian girls on the border, by mistake I gather. Their bodies have been found in the Zambezi River. Apparently they were swimming in the river. Ian Smith blames the British and says he has evidence that they were British bullets fired by British automatic rifles. Chaos looms Dad!"

Caroline at Miengwe/Petamikwa Hill

Dik - Dik

B.D.

In June I took another young lady out to Miengwe in our MGB. On this occasion my enthusiasm led me into an inappropriate friendship with a slender, charming, magnetic extrovert who was looking to spice her life up a bit, she said, "with an adventure". Could she join me on a trip to Miengwe next time I went? We had previously been on a husbands and wives bush-whacking trip, including her, to climb the 'holy' hill, Petamikwa. This prominent wooded hill was the only one in an otherwise rolling Copperbelt terrain and hence had been proclaimed the refuge of the tribal ancestral spirits of the Lamba people. Lamba people never ventured there for fear of the *Imfwiti* and the Guardian, a huge black cobra that dwelt under the rock. However Jo and I had discovered some very ancient Bushman rock-paintings on Petamikwa Hill. "Is there any chance we could go and see your rock paintings, I will bring my camera?" my charming new friend enquired. "Brian, I have got the day off tomorrow."

Victoria Falls *The Smoke that Rises.*

Breakfast at Moshi o Tunya - Jo and Caroline

Jo 1974

Brian. 1974

She lived nearby us in Itawa where I had met her bird-watching in the Itawa dambo. I had a meeting scheduled at Miengwe for the morrow and so off we went with the wind in our hair, to Petamikwa Hill and a good fun climb, she told me her favourite song was *The First Time Ever I saw Your face* with Roberta Flack. I knew it well; intensely romantic; she started singing it. I realised that the Lamba people had a point about Petamikwa; *"Don't go there."*

Jo was teaching as usual and I later realised that I couldn't tell her about my climbing the hill with our neighbour's wife as it would appear as a secret-liaison and happy couples don't have secret-liaisons. I had danced with her, rapturously, at the Tennis Club Ball – another mistake. In the outcome, nothing was said, and yet Jo instinctively knew that I was deviating – "women know women" she said, and became nervous and sullen, "Brian, what's going on!" I think she guessed who it was. Luck prevailed for me, the lady left Zambia two weeks later.

Jo fearfully wrote a poem which I have kept: *My life is like a tiny door, that's ever open wide, my love is like an ever raging sea that swells with every tide, my soul is like a fresh grown rose that sparkles in the dew, these things are only possible, if I can stay with you.*

In 1948 I had dedicated my whole life and soul to Cicely Marriott, now nick-named Jo and I held to that, in the outcome, for sixty two years. Such a small carelessness became an indelible and painful mark on our love affair at that time. We suffered three weeks of strained silences and depression such as we had never experienced before and finally our Waterloo loomed; it was ABBA's Waterloo, which was to win the Eurovision Song Contest. ABBA swept us off our feet with their fruity, sexy harmony which brought us back together on the dance floor at the Flying Club Ball. First love lasts forever, of course it does.

23rd August 1973:   Luangwa Valley National Park.
Our 18 year old son Philip had arrived from England, now a school leaver, with an ambition to take Susan Wagstaff on an adventure in Luangwa Valley National Park. We agreed a plan. It was the end of the dry season when all the animals were crowding along the river. We put the roof rack on the Peugeot 204 for the jerry cans of petrol and four bed rolls. We tumbled out of our beds at at 5.30 am, bright as buttons and finally reached Luangwa River Bridge East of Lusaka en route for Chipata and so to face the usual road block by the Zambian Army. They were more like children dressed in khaki but toting high powered rifles. They demanded to hear our record player before allowing us to *"mtembeya"* – continue our journey. Philip's face was red with rage. I hurriedly tried to divert their interest by telling them I was an ex-soldier and I had always wanted a

record player but they were not allowed in the barracks in my day. They were talking to a soldier.

It had taken us eleven hours to reach Chipata town, a small pretty place with blood red flowering small trees of *Combretum,* obviously enjoying the limestone brown soils. Geomorphologic-ally speaking Chipata, and also its people, are homogenous with Malawi. This mistake was typically a British colonial, mathematical mind-set, regardless of human culture, thus leading to eternal human conflict. Another example of this is in Sudan where Bantu people of the south are eternally in conflict with Arab Muslims of the north.

The sun went down on a game of Scrabble at the Kapololo Farm Institute in Chipata with a background of 70's popular music including **Papa Joe** by Mike Chapman which Philip chorused as Papa Brian, on Phil's record player. We were joined by an American lecturer named Tom Tiffany who was quite a rocker too. The following morning over breakfast Tom was more serious, "What they need in this country are technicians, not foreign aid experts. Zambia is too academic minded, a chair and a desk is the ambition of upper level students. Yes, Chipata is a one-horse town alright, you drive 365 miles of nothing, you arrive, and you are out the other side wondering where the main part is, so you pull up, do a three point turn in the main street and return to look again."

It was silent Sunday. "Where are you from Tom?" enquired Philip.

"Minnesota. Politics and life are more normal in Minnesota than anywhere else in the States."

"It must be because you are near the Canadian border," quipped Jo. He didn't dispute that. He did speak lucidly about California however.

"Everything new that happens in the States starts in California. No-one has roots there and hell it's crowded in places but wild and beautiful in others. You should go there."

Monday morning we spent on a fruitless shopping spree.

The Luangwa Valley Wildlife Department were very efficient compared to the morons in the government office. They were expecting us, being an Honorary Wildlife Ranger and gave me a pass to stay in Game Wardens' Quarters in the valley. The 85 mile drive down to Luangwa Valley was hard on our Peugeot 204, and likewise the ferry approach. The ferry was hand hauled like our Machiya ferry and certainly not suitable for any projected tourist trade, likewise the hotel that we checked out for a drink. Mfuwe Lodge had no extra facilities like East African hotels did. There was no swimming pool, no music, no illuminated night arena of animals as one gets in Kenya, but the scenery was dynamic. In the evening the beautiful honey badgers raided the garbage bins in full lighting, quite unafraid. For some reason the Honey Badger is greatly feared by all creatures in the Park including, even, lions. There is something about the colours black and white in nature that deters predators and even pests in the case of Zebra, which do not suffer from tsetse fly. Predators avoid magpies in the UK whilst some butterflies mimic black and white The surrounding wildlife show was quite incredible for its variety, density and vitality. Night-time was a theatre of sounds of great variety. Hyenas came into our kitchen and rattled amongst the saucepans. Lions, we were told, had been in and eaten the hose off the petrol pump right up to the metal spring.

We met Philip Berry, an ex-government Game Warden who had now settled down working for Z.N.T.B., conducting tourists on safari in search of the 'big three'. His wife said she hated the life in the bush; where had we heard that before? It was from the first Park Warden of Ruaha National Park in Tanzania and an old friend, Steve Stephenson, whose wife, sadly, "left him to it".

After bedding down in the Warden's empty-quarter, we spent the next day exploring that other world; 3,500 sq. miles of pre-gunpowder wildlife. We were surrounded by such a variety of animals and birds in great numbers throughout the yellow dried out acacia-savannah. The landscape was fundamentally an alluvial valley of grey soils with sandy terraces and lagoons. *Acacia spirocarpa* is a common tree. *Acacia albida* being the 'lollipop' species that the elephants love shaking violently for its tasty seed pods. This was the height of the dry season when animals crowd the river valley for water having raised their young far away, in January through to May.

Cheetah on the plain

We loaded our two teenage prospective lovers, onto the roof of my car and set off with sunhats, binoculars and the odd bottle of sun-stroke preventative medicine prescribed by Tusker. We later ventured to trek in tall yellow grass, keeping an eye out for any naughty lions wanting to play. Visitors are allowed to walk in the Park when accompanied by a Wildlife Ranger. We disturbed a crocodile on a kill by the river and a leopard with an antelope carcass in a tree. A small bird was squawking loudly in the clutches of a hawk and we found a large white rhino's skull. In fact, it seemed to Philip and Sue at the time "the natural world seems to be all about avoiding being murdered." *Homo sapiens* seems to have had the same problem, except that the enemy has not been another species but his own.

We loved the *Kigelia* trees by the river as did the monkeys, but it seemed that the gorgeous large velvety flowers were what they liked to sample, not the massive sausages hanging from all the branches. They say you can rot down the hard cases and flesh off them and retrieve a big sponge, a loofah, for your ablutions.

At dusk we were treated to a parliament of hippos echoing across the valley, debating loudly about the merits of the activities of the various different social unions, and where they should go on the river bank for an evening gorge of vegetation. Sometimes a rather nasty snorting erupted over some troublesome 'teenager' with his eyes on a not available young female. Some old males exhibited a giant gape of killer teeth, long enough to crunch a dug-out canoe in half. The males are quite fast too, like a U-boat at full speed coming towards you across the lagoon

"Shall we go for a swim?"

"I don't think so."

Recorded in Tanzania 2016:

Buffalos kill 7 people every year.
Lions kill 500 people every year.
Hippos kill 800 people every year.
Spiders kill 5000 people every year.
Scorpions kill 7000 people every year.
Snakes kill 10000 people every year.
Guess what?
Mosquitoes kill 2.7 million people every year.
The smallest are the deadliest.

Two Serval Cats dropped from a tree in front of our car. This very rare cat is very beautiful, larger than a domestic cat with longer legs, which act as springs enabling it to leap high and descend from above upon its victim, as if it were, from the sky.

Serval Cat

My hobby of sketching bird species was interrupted by a herd of black Cape Buffalos crossing our path. The vast numbers, amidst rising dust, took ten minutes to pass. The bulls weighed half a ton of prime beef. Why is it that the Africans never domesticated the buffalo as was the case in India and South East Asia? Domestic cattle in Africa are not native and hence they suffer from serious diseases and pests which buffalo are resistant to – famously the dreaded tsetse fly. I have read in books by explorers and hunters from late Victorian times that Africa from Cape Town to Nairobi was densely populated by wildlife like Luangwa is today. Maybe that is why the buffalo were not domesticated. Muzzle loading rifles had little impact but that all changed with breach loaders, rifled barrels and now automatic illegal Kalashnikovs.

A herd came strolling across our track, taking 43 minutes to pass; I counted 920 including probably 20% calves. The train must have been well over a mile long. Philip Berry told us "Buffalo are a major feature of the eco-system in the valley because of their grazing capacity; there are three such herds in the area." Imagine if such herds were not God's property but owned by some rancher, he would have to be a multi-multi-millionaire.

African larder

At 6.00 am the next day, we set off in search of the king of beasts. I called up to my scouts on the car roof, "Look over there in the tall grass." They did not believe me at first but the lion was pale yellow, barely visible in the pale yellow grass, even its eyes were golden colour. Pale Yellow seemed to be the in-colour; even the crocodiles were yellowish green. Wild-lifers say that only 8 out of 10 hunts are successful and the males leave it to the females if they can. Wild dogs are cleverer and rarely fail to make a kill. Lions rest for 20 hours a day in the 35 degree heat and hunt at night. They can see in the dark.

Five elephants waded in the lagoon by our Rest House, swinging lazily great bunches of rhizomatous long grass to shake off the water cabbages that carpet the lagoons and are presumably, not as tasty as they look.

We found an eroded bank by the river, perforated with hundreds of holes. This was one of Luangwa's famous sights, swarms of Carmine Beaters in their bright crimson plumage with duck egg blue rump and crown. Their bold black eye stripe attracts the human eye.

Passing in the car by a bank, about the height of our roof squatters, attracted the eye of a disapproving young bull elephant who charged down upon the terrified lovers, trumpeting loudly or should I say screaming; such a high pitch. I grabbed my camera and did get a slightly out of focus shot of him, much to the disgust of my roof squatters. "Dad, what are you doing? REVERSE."

Well, I know he was only showing off, much as Philip does when he gets a squash racket in his hand. Tembo, the more appropriate African name, did a reverse and stood his ground in the shade. I kept my eye on his eye whilst he sniffed the air flowing from my passengers, his huge ears flapping, his tusks threateningly catching the sunlight. The minutes ticked by. I pipped my little French hooter twice, which seemed a bit feeble after his trumpeting ferocity. He suddenly came again, marching out into the sunlight; head high at first, then trunk down between his legs which means business. I decided to proceed rather quickly down a side track, my roof squatters hanging onto the roof rack, feeling intimidated or should I say scared to death.

Chocolate elephants.

Look out !

Philip.

Luangwa Valley N.P. 1973

In the
Luangwa

Phil and Sue   Luangwa River

In the afternoon heat Jo and I sat in the little boat in the lagoon admiring the Lily Trotters. It was funny how they came so close with us at water level. A huge flock of guinea fowl came gliding low across the water and settled in the trees making my trigger finger wiggle.

The next day I gave the car keys to Phil and suggested he drove while Jo and I could sit on the roof in the breeze. Philip disturbed a herd of hippos that came running across his track giving me a good camera shot. We ended up at Mfuwe Lodge looking for beer. There wasn't any. I had a word with the Lodge Manager Ken Mukumbi who told me it was a four day round trip for their truck to Lusaka. "We'll get a plane soon."

Philip loved fishing and his efforts in the mighty Luangwa River had so far proved disappointing. Then suddenly the day before we left, he caught a huge barbel on a chunk of meat. It almost pulled him into the river; it was 36" in length and weighed 20 lbs. The Ranger told us that one had been caught five feet long and that they were known to attack women and children washing at the water's edge. So one might say they were omnivorous! I believe that this fish is the same as the one in Lake Kashiba in Mpongwe that was reputed to eat people with its huge flat gaping mouth and hard skull adorned with filaments.

5th September 1973
Departing from Luangwa today we had 540 miles to drive. We checked out of Mfuwe Lodge. Philip Berry's beautiful wife revealed herself in a black bikini on the veranda – no chance of getting overweight in Luangwa! After six hours thrashing through dry, soft sand, over cobbled clay river beds and up steep banks climbing out of river valleys, and then surmounting granite hills in dry, dead-looking *Mopani woodland* desolation, we finally arrived at a tarmac road. We could now step up to 80 mph of traffic-less heaven, that is except for the occasional goat. Crossing the lower Luangwa River by the new bridge caused annoying, frustrating delay and one could not contemplate taking tourists that way to Luangwa National Park. Those boys with guns could easily raise the temper of a less tranquil person than me; I can imagine some volatile heavy-weight blowing up the bridge in retaliation, it would be very easy actually. These soldier boys' mentality reminded me of the mentality of the borstal boys that we employed on our pig farm in Nottinghamshire years ago. These soldiers wanted to see every item in our luggage. They shook them in the air, especially ladies underwear, jewellery, passports, cameras, binoculars and tried them all out, even my Ranger handcuffs. I was tempted.

We arrived at Kachalola at 4.30 pm, the end of a pretty desolate Province. Getting dark at 6.00 pm we decided not to chance the main road to Ndola, 385 miles with drunken truck drivers, and invested 24 kwacha in the local 'hotel'. There was no room service as such, despite the 10% service charge, and food was 'mealy-meal'. Sue and Phil were asleep by 8.30 pm; in separate rooms.

Sue, Phil and Jo said how much they had enjoyed the holiday. Taking Sue back home meant collecting our 'senior' rabbit from Nancy Wagstaff's rabbit family. Our rabbit had also enjoyed its holiday. We were told that he had enjoyed two swims in their pool, so we now had a "baptised rabbit". "In what faith?" Sue enquired, "The church of the Holy Wag!" The rabbits were pulled out of the pond by their tails.

22nd September 1973

Sue joined in again for a safari to Chief Lesa's area for land surveying. Over the weekend we trekked the 4 miles down to Inampamba Lake. Our Peugeot 204 had acquired a second puncture hence Phil was left to exercise his initiative with "our lousy South African hot patches." He was tormented by sweat bees in the extreme heat. These tiny creatures head for human ears and nostrils for moisture. He eventually put out a bowl of water from our caravan and that drew them away.

Meanwhile Jo, me and Sue reached that great crack in the limestone landscape and pushed out in our inflatable canoe. It was very hot indeed and refreshing to paddle up and down, looking into the clear blue water below for fish. Even though the lake was 20 ft. below normal, the lake seemed bottomless. Limestone sidewalls were sheer up to the cloudless sky, hence no bilharzia snails or indeed access for any other crawly creatures. The nearest human habitation was ten miles away. Occasionally Jo and I would visit alone over a week-end and revel in the isolation and the purity of the lake and its surroundings, bathing and strolling naked in the heat.

We lay refreshed at dusk after Phil had joined us having driven to the lake, on the stony pavement. We later saw a satellite appearing to collide with Venus, an omen perhaps? We became enveloped in a globe of stars, so typical of 'Wild Africa' after dark. We lit a fire to cook our sausages. Phil was telling us that in England they had legislated for equality of women, so he reckoned that the day was not far off when Sue would have to repair the punctures whilst he went fishing! Jo said she did not agree with that legislation, not just because she objected to doing dirty, mechanical jobs but that it was demeaning for women to compete with men.

Philip was due to return to England in late September, having left school. He now faced the challenge of further education and where to live between times. It seemed likely that Jo's sister Jean in Fawley, Hampshire would step in and help, hence Jo was booked to fly home with Philip and Sue. Jo's school had been enjoined by a teacher named Liz Smith whose husband Derek had replaced the Falconers at R.C.M, they having joined a World Bank Project in Lesotho, Southern Africa. Hence Jo's class would be well cared for in Liz's house during her absence in England.

"Where would you like to live Philip?" He was dreaming of Luangwa Valley, singing:-

> *"Oh give me a home, where the buffalo roam*
> *Where the deer and the antelope play;*
> *Where seldom is heard a discouraging word*
> *And the skies are not cloudy all day."*

It strikes me that men in their forties are near the peak of their mental capacity, physical capacity and prowess. I had a month on my own after Jo left to visit family in the U.K. The Swedish lady who accompanied us to the airport was friendly with us, particularly because she was English born and married to a Swedish gentleman whom was away in Sweden. She accompanied me back home and settled down for the evening after our houseboy made our lunch. What to do?

What did happen that month was a round of Swedish home invitations for me and a dancing banquet in the town for all the Swedish and "Brian the Brit". The Swedish ladies were no beauty queens. Swedes are, I suppose, a fairly rugged lot on the whole but there was one! At the dinner table I wished that she would talk to me, sitting opposite like a classic portrait of Venus, but she remained aloof. That was not the case with the tumultuous rest. They whirled me round the dance floor; really sexy to dance with; it was not fair. I think in retrospect that it was all a plot, to be my un-doing.

At the next P.D.C. meeting the Vice President was in attendance. He advised me that His Excellency required me to visit Lilongwe in Malawi and send him an appraisal of the new World Bank Integrated Rural Development Project there. "He will send you a Mercedes car with driver next week. The driver will carry a letter of introduction for the Manager." I have to admit that I used this privileged event to contact a couple of old friends, the Chief Accountant and the Chief Game Warden of Malawi, David Ansty and sound them out for any potential vacancies in National Parks for when my Contract came up for renewal, next year in May 1974.

Jo returned to the fold, after six weeks with her children and family in England. It was strange how lovers parted become more and more desperate for each other's reunion and yet stepping off that plane at Ndola Airport we were quite formal with shyness. Jo was excited and to 'break the ice' began telling me about the children and everything they did together. She produced a record of 'our tune' *Night and Day* by Cole Porter. How perennial that tune is, like a historical legend, like the Bible, a story of love eternal. For us, when we became engaged, it was overwhelmingly romantic; those binding phrases produced an ageless commitment to each others' welfare that in the outcome carried us through many difficulties and dangers over twenty four years in Africa. It was that film that sealed our love together when I left for military service at the end of the War. And now? *"When You're in Love With a Beautiful Woman"* by Dr Hook.

"Hmm..... How about coffee, Jo?"

"Let's skip the coffee."

CHAPTER SEVEN

1974

This was to be the year of change. My contract terminated in May. We had no other home to go to in England, so we decided to go to Japan where our intrepid daughter Caroline was now living with her shipping agent husband Iain. Contract renewals in the post-colonial era depended upon the host government requesting the British government for the services of that Officer. After Japan, we would visit the rest of our family in the U.K. and twiddle our thumbs apprehensively. Our married son Richard had now graduated in Hotel Management and was employed by the NHS at the new Queen Elizabeth Hospital in Birmingham whilst nineteen year old, betrothed, Philip was a penniless student at Stockport College of Technology.

Hence Jo and I, at the age of 44, were faced with a childless life in Africa but financially responsible for ourselves only, we hoped. Our declared purpose in marrying after the War was to create a family of six children, but husband Brian fell prone to his parsimonious nature after three, so we now needed to conjure up further ambitions for the next forty years or so.

It had been my ambition to persuade the chiefs to hand over 'their land' to the government by the end of this, my second contract. In the outcome, 15,000 square miles had now been agreed and declared State Land. The chiefs had lost their status over vast tracts of the landscape, as had happened with the nobility in the U.K. after the two recent wars, but the African chiefs still held sway over their tribes-people and retained political influence in the House of Chiefs, since their native followers would vote according to their chief's wishes. The One Party State candidates for election were obliged to exercise favourable influence over the chiefs and their people in the constituencies.

I was faced with reconnaissance soil surveys for my Mpongwe Development Zone plan, as well as delineating the zonal boundary for legislation. A German Aid team, Agro-unit Hydrotechnic, for the Munkumpu Crop Research Station, arrived for that soil survey.

No longer faced with supporting our children - theoretically, we decided to give more attention to our ambitions to save the wildlife of this vast country. Those Somali tanker drivers were a challenge; their business was selling oil and buying copper bars for loading under the tank for the return journey. This task required stalwart enterprising men. However, as history records, Somalis are not just good looking but enterprising in acquiring money for modern weapons for warfare. Elephant ivory from Zambia was much in demand in the Arab world and became a means to start a war in Somalia, via poached Luangwa Valley elephants and the hell-run. Somali drivers did not need to trek across country to Luangwa National Park for ivory but simply paid African hunters to do the job for them. I would need African Ranger back-up to effectively operate road blocks to catch them. Hence my plan to take over the local branch of the Wildlife Conservation Society of Zambia as Chairman and to select two suitable candidates for training by the Game Department and have them Gazetted as legal Wildlife Rangers. However, they would have to be paid by our local branch of WLCSZ, hence a long term enterprise of fundraising and management which became a gigantean new lifestyle hobby for Jo and I.

16th May 1974. Travelling on leave - *Nairobi*
After a nostalgic and romantic flight from Ndola across those familiar Tanzanian plains and lakes, we *Jambo'd* our way to the New Stanley Hotel. Nairobi was fabulous. Can there be any city in the world that was such a joy to be in, in 1974. Our schedule would take us to many historic cities; Athens, Istanbul, Singapore, Hong Kong, Bangkok, Tokyo, yet our favourite would remain Nairobi.

We went up to Limuru in Kenya to visit our Tanga friend who helped me build that water fountain in the middle of the dance floor at the Tanga Yacht Club Ball, nine years ago. Laurie Bamford had exchanged his ex-Bluebell Girl wife of Tanga days, for another, and lived a *Happy Valley* family life in an idyllic spot overlooking the Rift Valley. They seemed happy to settle in Kenya and we could see why. Laurie took us to the Country Club where we met other ex-Tanzanian friends and swapped stories about people we mutually knew. East and Central Africa is a small place for Europeans.

18th May 1974 – *Izmir*
Our arrival at Izmir airport, or should I say airfield, from our stay in Athens, was treated with open mistrust by numerous armed young militia. Their stern faces were unwelcoming. The Grand Ephesus Hotel in the central square was desolately empty and our presence at a dining table seemed to be verging on an embarrassment to the staff. With the language barrier we felt that we must have put a foot wrong somewhere and felt like intruders. In the morning we awoke to a fanfare of trumpets and a military parade in the square below. It transpired that this was the day the Turks celebrated the repulsion of the much hated Greek invasion forces, a la Cyprus today. We had arrived from Athens, hence our cool reception.

Thank heavens we found an interpreter, a dusky Turkish damsel who needed money for her studies and intended to enter the tourist business. She kindly offered to show us the Roman town of Ephesus, Salcuk Museum, and Kusagasi seaside resort. We had learnt that women were no longer in purdah in Turkey thanks to the 1924 revolution. The revolutionary leader, Ataturk who was still, understandably greatly revered, was on the coinage and in every square.

The farmers were already harvesting potatoes, cherries and strawberries. There must be a great potential for supplying the European Union markets from Turkey's vast fertile land; what a contrast to the dry rock and concrete landscape we experienced in Greece. If only the men would stir from the shade where they whiled away the hours discussing how to beat the Greeks and instead, join forces with their hard-working wives and horses and develop their agriculture. Jo and I felt that in Turkey we had one foot in Africa and one in Europe.

*20th May 1974 – **The Ephesians***

It was a wonderful day spent immersed in the beginnings of western civilisation. We strolled down Marble Street and Harbour Street, passing the remains of fish shops with their fish ponds for keeping their wares fresh in the hot climate. As our footsteps echoed across the pavements of the city, it seemed that we had the company of a 'durable pair of sandals', those of a simple man whose words outlasted the broken marble columns and statues of famous men, lining the streets. His words as eternal as the surrounding hills, the man whose arm and a skull fragment we saw later in the Selcuk Museum, was John the Baptist.

We took our ease for a while in the silence of the amphitheatre, trying to visualize the hub-bub of graceful Roman citizenry, merchants, traders, artisans and administrators escorting their wives and children along the line of shops and beggars. Down in the square we imagined 'our man in sandals' might have attracted a crowd of lesser mortals to listen to his worship of Goddess Diana at the great temple on the hill. The shoppers would have murmured about the need to act more positively against the disruptive elements in their civilized society.

*20th May 1974 **Istanbul***

A local plane took us north and a taxi man found us 'digs' in a private house where we learned to enjoy Turkish breakfasts with olives and cream cheeses, and tea in a small glass without milk. The High Street was jammed solid with big old cars so we walked around the glorious mosques and the Grand Bazaar where I got a pair of the latest flared trousers made to fit, overnight. Jo also got fitted out with a glamorous bright red jacket made of camel skin. Also overnight she had her Tanzanite stone, obtained from the Tanzania Trade Stand at Ndola Trade Fair, mounted into a ring. Istanbul was an exciting place, and inexpensive.

Hotel foyer

'Guests are invited to take advantage of the chambermaid.'

At Topkapi Palace door

Topkapi Palace Guards.

Istanbul Grand Bazaar

Fresh fish and chips

"Cup of tea Sir?"

The biggest emerald in the world

116

27th May 1974 – **Singapore**

Singapore was a tremendously easy-going place with beautiful young women who ate you up if you responded to their hungry glances like the snake-charmer we bumped into.

I was interested in the identity of his very large black snake. The turbaned black Indian, however, saw me as a customer. He advised me that it was a mamba. My look of disbelief that it could be brethren of the deadliest snake in Africa, spurred him on and he said, "I tell you, Sahib, this my friend. He velly musical, no pwoblem. Watch." He proceeded to play his bulbous pipe to charm the reptile. "Now you try Sahib," he said, suddenly stepping towards me. He swung the serpent round my shoulders and handed me the pipe which I hastily blew, madly! It coiled round my arms and neck in a friendly embrace. Jo took a photograph and in haste, double exposed it. There was, however, no need for haste. In fact any sudden movement might have found me with a 'strike on my hands'!

Singapore old and new

There was, by now, a sizeable audience watching the Englishman for any sign of timidity and I felt committed to a brave face. In any case I had difficulty in finding the reptile's head and could not therefore gauge the look in its eye! With two hands upon the pipe, trying to raise a tune that was in the mamba pop charts, I had no choice but to wait upon the Indian's favour to rescue me. If that photo comes out OK, I shall be revered amongst my African survey staff in Ndola and even by Chikoti!

5th June 1974

Jo and I did all the things that visitors do in verdant, humid, crowded Singapore where people lived on top of one another in spectacular tower blocks. The population statistics for Singapore are 18,645 people per sq. mile, which compares with UK 650, Zambia 40, Japan 339. We enjoyed cabaret evenings, horror tableaux of Chinese tortures in the Gier Balm Gardens, the Thieves Market in a rickshaw. The Oriental Dance Theatre was rather a let-down when they washed off their star-spangled eyes. In the following days we visited the fabulous Orchidarium, and travelled over the border into Malaysia to Johor and the rubber plantations. The two things that stuck in minds were the friendly black mamba and those 44,000 white grave stones on a hillside of, mainly Australian, soldiers who died fighting the Japanese invaders. Now that we were leaving for a friendly liaison with the Japanese, we swore that we would not forget those men who stayed behind so that we could choose. Our next stop was Bangkok market to purchase some solid gold bracelets, and then Hong Kong.

6th June 1974 – *Tokyo*

After the most luxurious flight we had ever experienced, our Cathay Pacific Jumbo touched down for a joyful reunion with our daughter Caroline. After all the hassle with begging porters at Hong Kong and Singapore, the large notice at Haneda Airport announcing "Tipping is forbidden." was a welcome relief. "They mean what they say here," said Iain as the porter loaded our luggage into his Toyota Crown. We drove through the crowded city of 13 million people, "Larger than London" Iain said, "Japan's population of 120 million must be amongst the most crowded countries in the world."

We arrived at their luxury apartment in Akasaka and dropped our shoes at the doorway in Japanese-style. Chiki, Caroline's tailless fluffy white cat, greeted us. The wild Japanese Macaque, a red faced baboon is also tailless. Everything is odd in Japan. Chiki was born to an indoor destiny and now had no place to go outdoors at all. Few cats have gardens in Tokyo. The daily opening of the veranda windows was Chiki's '*New World Symphony*' of scents and sounds. Chiki's other passion was flower arranging. She purred around the vases when Caroline was out, often consuming the blooms, leaving a vase full of stalks. Chiki had a serious neurosis problem with Iain's quadraphonic stereo unit. She hid deep inside one of the high up kitchen wall units when Iain flooded the atmosphere with multi-various wave lengths, especially with his favourite, *B.J.Thomas.*

7th June 1974

Caroline carried off her new lifestyle with aplomb; how different to her life on the farm in Norfolk as a child and in the African 'bush'. She had learned the pearl trade when living in Hong Kong and had learned silk-painting and Ikebana at classes in Tokyo. We complimented her upon her efficient household management, and her adept socializing with all races and social strata despite the incomprehensible language. Caroline is totally devoid of any race or class consciousness, which I hope reflects well upon her upbringing.

Ikebana by Caroline

Caroline loving life in Japan

"Kwa heri." "See you in Seattle, goodness knows when."

A word about I*kebana*: Like everything else in Japan, flower arranging is not flower arranging in the Western sense but an artistic expression of mood, or even a message to a guest or relative due to arrive in the house, using flowers, stems, leaves and a particular style of vase. The expression may take a long time to ponder, not just, "Oh, I must just pop these flowers in a vase." Caroline studied this art over a period of many months.

Despite her success in creating a good home and being devoted exclusively to the welfare of her husband, destiny had not rewarded them with any children which had been Caroline's ardent desire since her marriage in Mombasa at the age of 19. They told us that their next move would be to Seattle USA where "life will be easier". Would their luck change?

8th June 1974. The Ginza
Caroline did her 'Guide Dog for the Blind' act and took us by bus to the Tokyo Ginza for shopping. There were lots of 'dwarf' peasant-type women on the buses, bringing produce from rural areas. I gathered that they were fairly typical of a generation subjected to the medieval land tenure system, abolished by General MacArthur in 1946 when the aristocracy were 'asset stripped'. Nothing typifies the political transformation in Japan more than the contrast between these older wives on the buses and the younger wives in the glitzy Ginza shops. Unsurprisingly, we noticed that the Japanese expressed dislike of Americans but conversely liked the British who "taught them how to make cars." We did not need a Visa to enter Japan, unlike the Americans.

The Ginza is the 'West End' of Tokyo, except that they close the area off to traffic on the main shopping day of the week, Sunday, there being a six day working week. Sunday, tables were set out in the streets for refreshments; anything to delay the big spenders around the shops. Everyone looked happy and well dressed, including the pretty children who sat obediently on the kerbside to devour their ice creams. Japanese streets were squeaky clean and the reason is that the Japanese are horrified by litter. You might respond, "Well we don't like litter either, it's those others." In Japan, "the others" are themselves. In their intensely disciplined society, the children have to clean their schools themselves on a rota system from day one. The money saved is spent on teaching staff.

From our eye level, the sea of heads stretched from wall to wall, resembling a black carpet. We reached a Square, where there was a crowd of chattering boys that attracted us to examine the stall selling pets. Most popular were the hermit crabs, clattering about in a bowl in their 'squatter' shells. Little cages contained cockroaches and crickets and sometimes birds. There was a puppy, a rarity in Japan. Entering a store, a beautiful girl dressed in a kimono bowed and explained the layout of the premises and wishing us "Happy shopping" made us feel like a Duke and Duchess.

I had one very amusing dream; I imagined our 6'2" son, Philip was with us in Japan, shopping in the Ginza for an evening dress suit, the last thing that Philip would ever do, being the easy-going casual rebel student. His height and wild curly hair could not be allowed to deter us from supporting this accommodating turnaround of events. However, the giggling crowds of little people were too much for us as he stood in the store, in the largest size they could find; a bit like Worzel Gummage, with short sleeves, bow tie, top hat, bushy hair protruding, and wearing dark-tinted spectacles! Philip always enjoyed an audience. We retreated to a shop the other side of the arcade. Such is the drama of dreams! In England Phil's fiancé Susan Wagstaff was now working in London thus threatening their relationship.

30th June 1974

Jo and I ventured to use the Metro on our own. The Metro carried 4,000 people every three minutes. It was so crowded in the city that coats were pressed against the glass windows, but we were almost alone by the time we reached the docks area. In no time at all, we were arrested with no Passports and ended up at a Police Station. We used the Police phone to call Iain to come to our rescue with Passports; it was a long wait. The policemen were prepared apparently and plied us with smiles and luxurious green tea, in lieu of conversation.

In the evening we went to a restaurant again. Japanese cooking is exquisite, always small portions and no haste. This time we had delicious tempura crab, followed by sukiyaki (beef) with butter/garlic knobs and sauces. The waiter presented each of us with a hot stone upon which to cook the marbled, finely-sliced Kobe beef, ourselves.

Caroline cooking Japanese style

<u>*2nd July 1974*</u>
We were reading The Times; the U.K. news seemed awful, so many political chickens had come home to roost for the Labour Government! Inflation was 20%, the trade deficit was running at £1 billion per month and the Stock Market was at its lowest for 50 years. Our personal savings were worthless, property was the only secure investment and we did not have any of that. Should we ever be able to live in the U.K. again?

I got a super photograph of Caroline sitting in amongst her prehistoric ancestors on a tableau at the museum. I managed to avoid arrest this time, just! Caroline took us to the All Girls' Review at Kokusai Theatre. The performances were very refined and exhilaratingly feminine! One troupe of girls danced in pale green kimonos with red sashes and fans and another girl danced a fire-dance to a rock tempo, dressed in red ostrich plumes and fans. After the interval, the play involved burning down a mansion on stage!

3rd July 1974. Nippon Manners

Social customs in Japan are not easy to get used to, everything is captivatingly opposite: Shopping day is Sunday (closing day in England in 1974), because of the six day working week. When introduced, you shake hands with yourself and bow. Wives help husbands on with their coats. Cats have no tails and gardens have no flowers. Wine (sake) is served hot and fish is eaten raw. When you bathe you scrub up outside the bath tub so as not to soak in dirty water. You leave your wife at home when you are invited out to supper. You marry the wife's family. The word 'plan' does not exist in the Japanese language, Tokyo is absolute total chaos. When you finally die, after a lifespan greater than in the western world, "probably from drinking too much coffee", the mourners will wear white and you might even be worshipped. Our over-whelming impression of the Japanese was their kindness, politeness and self-discipline. They have an overwhelming desire, often expressed, for peace in the world. This arises from their massive casualties in the war viz Okinawa, 240,000, Nagasaki, millions.

A wealthy friend named Enosan took us to one of the original Geisha Houses which was a unique privilege with charming conversations, music and dancing. My photograph says it all.

Street festivals take place every weekend, staged by the shopkeepers to attract trade. Colourful water gardens, immaculately kept, are numerous and serve as refuges in the frequent earthquakes.

Endita Mukwai

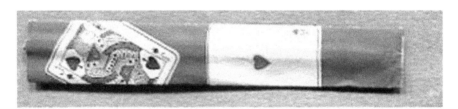

Secret Geisha Message.
For Brian. __

Water gardens make earthquake refuges
Acres of Irises

Enoshima town

Enter here: COME IN.   Moving Gorilla will grab you.

We took the wonderfully efficient 160 kph Bullet Train to the ancient one thousand year old capital city of Kyoto. This train was already of an HS2 standard back in 1974. The Japanese have been Zen Buddhists since ancient times with some Shintu thrown in and some 1,500 temples prevail in this rainy forested city. With the language problem, we were unsure which capital they were referring to, Kyoto or Tokyo. Certainly in Tokyo temples and shrines are also abundant and an active feature of life today. The philosophy of healthy spiritual and physical well-being was a common topic of conversation with Japanese friends. We rather liked being advised that the human body becomes rejuvenated at the age of 61 years. The one phrase we learned to use constantly was *domo arigato*, meaning thank you very much.

The Bullet Train [HS2 in 1974]

Going to Kyoto the old capital city

Villages along the line of rail

The old capital Kyoto - Jo needed her camel skin.

Kyoto

Water Gardens everywhere.

Love messages

Ivory carving - ancient skill. They don't know about elephants.

All schools same uniform

Zen Bhudist monk in training.

The Bhudist has run away

Zen Holy Water

The Kabuki Theatre was incomprehensible. It was said to be the Shakespeare of Japan. No Comment. The tea ceremony was more of a one-act play, taking an hour to drink a cup of green tea with two ladies, gorgeously dressed in kimonos, was a unique experience in refined manners and minimal conversation. We were amused by the ceremonial washing of your weekly wages in a holy fountain flowing from a sculptural work of the White Dragon, the most revered of all spirits. I was told by Machiba San, our English-speaking driver, upon learning of my birth day, that I was a White Dragon and a "very special person". Actually Jo knew that already.

Machiba San says Brian is a White Dragon = Oct 1928

Our Driver

この黄金浄水で
お金を洗い清め
財宝がふえるよう
お祈りしましょう
奉納世話人

Wash your money here - the White Dragon

"Take me to London please."

With Kilimanjaro in mind, we set off for Mount Fuji, its snow shining invitingly in the summer sunshine. Machiba San – San means Mister – drove us up the first three quarters of the way to a restaurant and car park. One hopes that the Tanzanians do not decide that they would attract more tourists for Kilimanjaro, by building a road up. The final third of the 'strenuous climb' was by horse and carriage, up to a cap of loose black gravelly cinders. We had to walk the rest, blanketed by snow, although a clear pathway ensured that you could not get lost. At the summit, there was a telephone kiosk for us to phone our friends. There wasn't a line to Ndola Zambia unfortunately, although I suppose that today one could do that by satellite anyway.

After a long stay in Japan we popped over to England to await news of my contract renewal for Zambia. We rang the door bell of Richard and Ann's house in Birmingham. The sheer joy of it was immense, and after quenching our thirst on Richard's home-made wine he declared;

"Don't retire here Dad, this country's bankrupt and everyone is leaving. It looks like Britain might even be leaving the Commonwealth and becoming part of Europe."

"What!"

"Ann says she is going to vote for the new Party; what's it called Ann?"

"***The Action Party***" she said "I have got a note here: *Action for Change by Ralph Nadar;* increase the working week to six days with all pay on the sixth day tax-free, to get production up. Start a Buy British campaign to reduce imports. Reduce purchase tax on home produced goods and make credit available. Nationalise building land to stop speculators and keep building land at farmland prices like the U.S.A. and Eire. Take all possible steps to encourage tourism. Stop immigration completely. Expel all Irish nationals after three months' notice; and after that, IRA bombing to be halted by Eire; as a deal with the U.K. for the return of their employment opportunities. Also; stop recruiting teachers under the age of thirty."

"Wow! I like that."

We later hired a mobile home on the bank of the River Avon in Christchurch for a warm family get-together by the sea-side, and a bit of fishing for Philip. We needed that!

3rd October 1974. ***Back to Zambia.***

Having 'abandoned' our children in bankrupt Britain, we were happy to be back in our lovely house in Ndola in bankrupt Zambia. The returns from exported copper were well below the cost of imports. The closure of the border to the south by Prime Minister Iain Smith of Rhodesia, a man of the Sir Roy Welensky ilk, had a devastating impact on Zambia. The nation known historically as Northern Rhodesia was orientated south 100%, with no historical connections to the north at all. Africa is a very big place!

Zambia was now obtaining its oil supply by road tanker from the Mediterranean Arab States via Somalia, Kenya and Tanzania, down to our Great North Road; 640 miles of gravel surface prone to rainfall erosion, consequently called The Hell Run. The Arab States accosted President Kaunda of Zambia with the threat of cutting off their oil supply unless they evicted the Israelis of Kafulafuta and Kafubu Settlement Scheme "within 24 hours." This arose as a result of the Israeli/Arab war of 1973/4. It was done by the time we visited the scheme after our leave. We found 500 starving pigs; a sad sight for pig lovers like Jo and I. The tragedy was not really the smallholder farmers fault, but it was the fault of the concept of co-operative farming. If one is running a farm on borrowed money, one needs to have some understanding of the way the world of finance works. Farming in any part of the world is such hard work that survival can only be achieved, in my opinion, by individual enterprise for individual gain. It was, after all, the failure of communal production of food that brought down the Soviet Empire. The Kafulafuta/Kafubu Co-operative 'empire' was destined to fail anyway because 'the books' were kept entirely in Hebrew. Having researched Israeli documentation of their historical relations with Africa on the internet, I can find no mention of this failed project.

We were now enjoying Zambia's relaxing and expansive atmosphere backed up by the 70's fabulous popular music to dance to every Saturday's 'clubbing' night. However a new stumbling block to progress in my official duties had arisen. A new incumbent Planning Officer, with glowing paper qualifications from Bangladesh, had appeared from nowhere and was occupying my office block in the Agriculture Department. He was in cohorts with our new Provincial Agricultural Officer Chikoti and his native doctor 'advisor'. This new man, knew nothing whatsoever about the job, and refused to hand over my offices upon my return from leave. Such was a hazard of working in post-colonial Africa. I would need to look after myself and sort this out. My protector was the British High Commission, which had dismally failed us in Tanzania during a crisis of recognition. My expatriate technical boss in Lusaka, Norman Beaumont, was my only hope of retaining sanity. My being of an emotionally 'cool' temperament, Chikoti was afraid of me, I assumed nothing hotter than a calculating expression, in his presence. I was happy to establish myself at home temporarily, with a telephone and my senior staff enjoying morning coffee with me each day to keep things going.

8th October 1974

Jo and I conducted the President around Miengwe Settlement Scheme yet again! We now had 165 family farmers. The Press were there of course, Zambia TV, and a Swedish film company. The President worked in a trench laying domestic water supply pipes for three and a half hours without looking up. After the helicopters had left, we chatted with our new Volunteer-leader Frederick Aminoff and Jiri Novak, our refugee from the Czechoslovakia under Russian rule. In 1972 Frederick, 6feet 7inches tall, "Bwana Blue-gum," was also a refugee with a Russian immigrant background. Frederick said that he did not much care for the Swedes 'boorish' character and was considering moving south at the end of his contract. He said a book had been published in Sweden containing a full write-up on Miengwe Scheme "Swedish version" by Peter Borg, which was how he came to volunteer. We needed to relax after a stressful day. Once more to the Swedish sauna in the forest.

17th October 1974

I had persuaded the Ndola Rural District Council to hand over 20,000 hectares of land in the south of the now officially designated Mpongwe Development Zone, including some land of Chief Mwinuna to the Tobacco Board of Zambia. Walter Hartshoun was with us overnight from TBZ as well as Norman Beaumont, Vic Crust and Mr Nkhata, all from Lusaka HQ. Hence the prospect of well organised and extensive modern Tenant Growers Scheme for an export crop of Virginia Tobacco. So things were really moving in the Mpongwe area thanks to the determination of Jo and I over seven years of dogged persistence and the application of plain common sense, plus I should confess, a lot of academic study into the language of soil science to impress the egg-heads in the Government.

Nick Nielsen, sounds Scandinavian? Yes, Danish, a wild-haired Volunteer who had been organising the fencing of three thousand acre paddocks in an uninhabited area along the Congo border in the northwest region of the Province. Ngosa Ranching Scheme was my plan for retiring copper miners. At our meeting Nick told me that he planned to drive back to Denmark on his motorcycle! I supposed that it might be possible following the Somali truckers route to northern Kenya and then following the Nile from Uganda through Sudan. "You'll need a handgun, Nick."

21st October 1974. *My Birthday*

Jo and I met the Dutch and German soil surveyors at Munkumpu Agricultural Research Plot near Lake Kashiba, their names were Van Gessel and Dr Gruenberg. After a bit of technical chit-chat, the lure of Lake Kashiba's deep blue water drew all nationalities to its challenging depths whilst Brian caught a huge Bream for our planned birthday supper; the Lamba verdict; certain death. We drove to Miengwe to join the Swedes for supper, where our caravan now was. Some visiting Swedes instigated a beating of naked bodies with Eucalyptus branches in the sauna, "to add some zip". It was like a whole new lease of life, invigorating, refreshing, and hormonally stimulating. As I entered my 46th year I felt capable of anything.

8th November 1974

It was our 26th wedding anniversary and we were now alone and ready to face any challenge, not the least to be totally self-reliant. Jo was the most popular model in my photo studio, in black and white, with a 90-62-90 figure or 36-24-36 in colonial size. She posed in a wedding veil; actually a mosquito net. We later went to Kitwe to see a film called *Darwin Adventure* which was an interesting insight into life in our Victorian empire-building times, of rigid discipline, creative steam powered engineering, severe social stratification, and stern Christian doctrine. My family had lived at that time in Halifax for 500 years in a state of depravity; Jo's family had been farmers, prospering in East Sussex. We felt very glad of 'today'.

1974 had been a momentous year, having been to Japan, and to UK in search of our family. A Labour Government in the U.K. was elected with an overall majority of three. The 1970's decade was proving to be one of total economic chaos in Britain, and similarly in the U.S.A. The price of gold rose from $30 - $190 per ounce. The banks in the U.K. were offering 13% interest on one year fixed deposits. A lot of people sold-up their savings and bought gold Kruger Rands; tax-free in Jersey. The Stock Market 100 Share Index fell to 50. At the time of writing this in early 2018 the Footsie Index is 7,476.98. Unfortunately Zambia's wealth was not in gold but in copper, which was in reverse gear. The struggle continued; Chikoti told me that he knew what I had been saying about him in England when I was on leave and the British Embassy had been informed. Jo said, "You must be trembling in your shoes Brian."

CHAPTER EIGHT

1975

1974 went out under ever darker political clouds in the U.K., with inflation running at 20%. The trade deficit was breaking records month by month and famous companies were going bankrupt; Aston Martin, British Leyland, Burmah Oil. IRA terrorism continued unabated.

In Zambia the skies were less dark but the horizon was ominously grey, the nation was secretly looking south for its economic resolution. In our Department of Agriculture the situation was dire with development projects targeted at food production not being soundly managed under the grey cloud of Chikoti-ism, with me having to work from home.

"We are 46 years old Brian. What next? You and I fell in love when we were 14 and our plan to have six children to help with the farm turned out to be only three. Not very prolific are we. You are too parsimonious that's the trouble. How about making up the number NOW?

"We can't afford it Jo."

"There you go again. You are the biggest risk taker I have ever come across. Your work in Africa proves my point. If I was on the Pill I could make up your mind for you. Don't worry I'm not planning to do that again. Brian, just come back into the real world for a minute. You are stuck with Chikoti and no office; you have a commercial farming project in the offing, to feed the nation as they say, not a village. Where are we going?"

"I suggest; the bathroom."

"You do have a very determined nature; I'll say that for you."

"You mean a one-track mind."

"I didn't say that. You love bird watching I know; naked and feathered,."

"Right; that's where we're going next; conserving the natural world that we both love. Now that I've taken over the Ndola/Luanshya Branch of the Wildlife Conservation Society of Zambia, together with the zoo in the Trade Fair grounds, it's going to be a BIG job; for both of us."

"You mean I am starting another family after all, only with four legs each and self-made clothing. Not so easy as it sounds; they have their own code of behaviour that's the trouble. So, how big is my new family?"

"There are three baboons, a Serval Cat, a spiteful Caracal and a Cheetah; so far. There may soon be some rescued animals from our Ranger patrols."

Jo organised a trial film tour of the rural district entitled; "Conservation of Wildlife and Natural Resources." The physical effort was by my two new

Wildlife Rangers Adamson Lukuwa, Grey Mushitu and Mr Banda of Information Services mobile unit. The response was interesting; Mpongwe 849 people attended, Luswishi River 188, Mibenge F.T.C. 375, Chamushalila villages 446, Machiya 215, Kafulafuta 491, and Miengwe 316 – a total of 2,810. This indicated a positive route for spreading the word for a long term change of attitude to killing the few remaining wild animals for their skin, and meat. Wildlife films hence-forward became very popular. Mpongwe Farmer Training Centre had not run a course for 12 months, farmers always excusing themselves, "No transport Sir," yet 375 turned up for our film, on foot and bicycles..

We began putting on Tanzanian wildlife colour slide shows at the mine club and monthly wildlife films from South Africa at Ndola Cinema. Soon our membership began to climb thus requiring a very active and dedicated committee. A Secretary was appointed named Di Bushel who proved to be a dynamic character, extremely efficient and energetic to the dismay of the committee at times. I had occasion to visit her at home, out of town. I was shocked at the uncivilised state of their house. Her husband was an accountant earning good money and somewhat elevated in manner despite living in what, as an ex-farmer, I ventured to designate at the time, as a 'pig-sty' *with apologies to Di.* She had two children whom had the free run of the chaos; completely wild was my verdict, speaking as a wild-lifer.

Di was a volunteer, as we all were of course, and I depended upon her admirable energy and skill. At committee meetings we all had to learn tolerance of 'strong' language and forthright 'advice', in pursuit of 'the cause' Di's written English was actually very good, and a god-send for me in preparing my monthly Newsletter; *Get Out of Town,* which tended to contain long screeds of ornithology, flora, insectivore, and wildlife to look out for that month. Di made coffee for the committee too, although it was always a quiet guessing game as to what she made it with. We couldn't dodge consuming it despite her pint size mugs. One morning we were slogging through the minutes at her house, when she suddenly jumped up and said, "My God, I've forgotten the flan!" She came back with a bowl of lemon and egg white which had set solid, placed it on the table and whisked it up into slurry; "I hope the taste will prevail." she said. We all made our excuses.

I met another family of wild hooligan children. The father was an African doctor and his wife, who was English. They asked me to lend them two pairs of binoculars for their boys to go bird watching. I doubted we would get them back; another case of scatter-brain children. "If we'd had scatter brains on the farm our children would not have survived would they Jo."

"Brian, as I've said before, your whole attitude to family life has always been somewhat Edwardian. You expect everyone to keep in their place. A bit stuffy I'd say. Be less dominating; learn to say please sometimes."

That evening we were in the bedroom and Jo announced she was heading for her beloved bathroom. "If you vant to vatch, say please!" She knew she was on a winner there. She was right, of course about me being stuffy and I depended upon her socially to bring a ray of sunshine and laughter into the discourse. The room always lit up when Jo entered, but for me it was "and Brian came too." I did enjoy conversation but it needed to have a purposeful topic. I was fascinated by what was over the horizon not what we did yesterday.

Jo and I both went crazy on 1970's Pop, every Saturday night at one of the many Clubs in Ndola. It was part of our love affair and our *joie de vivre* in living in wildest Zambia. ABBA now led the rhythm explosion on the dance floor – they were so harmoniously different somehow. They had two upper levels of female harmony with a male voice below which made their music fruity and sexy. We remember *Dancing Queen* and *The Winner Takes it All*. The latter song was slightly sad. I suspect this was at the point when Agnetha divorced Borg.

We had discovered in our childless life, many new friends; British, African, Dutch, Persian, Swedish, Israeli and American.

We were close to the Congo border in the Copperbelt and Congolese filtered into Zambia selling their wares, principally oil paintings of modernistic style figures, and music. The Congolese Africans were heavily influenced by Belgian/French artistry in contrast to the Zambians who had suffered burdensome pressure from Afrikanerdom. The Congolese band playing at the hotel on Saturdays, was excitingly so non-Zambian, non-British, non-American but colourfully rhythmical and tunefully, dynamically, African.

Africans have a genetic talent for language, quickly learning English at Primary School in addition to their native tribal language. English is the national language in Zambia and when it comes to exercising their inborn talent for oratory, English is a rich and fertile field for educated leaders of men. His Excellency Dr Kenneth Kaunda could speak expressively and with depth of feeling, without notes, at great length. Any sense of flagging in his seated audience around the 'anthill' and he would suddenly shout "One Zambia!" and his startled listeners would shout back "One Nation!" He enjoyed immense status as the "Father of the Nation" and did so for 27 years. When meeting him personally, Jo and I found him friendly with no air of status; unassuming, and happy to enjoy Jo's easy entertaining conversation. I suppose we also had an affinity with his egalitarianism.

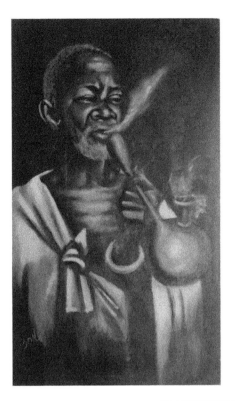

Congo drummer

1974

We played Mah-jong every Sunday evening with our good friends the Tysons. I was quite good at it being mathematically minded, making my presence a challenge, however, the endless banal chat about nothing in particular left me dreading Sundays, like sermons at Morning Song did when I was a teenager. Then, it was for me, a case of survival, the relieving factor being the rapport with the village girls; all the teenagers were in the choir in those days; we sang twice on Sundays, and practiced on Thursday evenings. I became a good Christian boy, at least "for the time being". Back in 1973 in Ndola we had entertained an elder of the Israeli team named David who told us that Jesus of Nazareth, being one of them, was ceremonially buried near the Mount of Olives.

Towards the end of the rains we were able to enjoy the swimming pools of our friends. Viewed from the air the blue pools were dotted all over the city, a by-product of the prosperity from copper mining not from my realm; Kafubu Dairy farm, family farmer schemes, cattle ranches &c., though much enjoyed by country yokels like Jo and I.

Despite my trauma with the academically over-qualified on paper Bangladeshi, occupying my office under the 'primitive' influence of Chikoti the PAO, I was now relaxing at home pending rescue. All my development schemes had come to a halt whilst I was on leave, the Swedish volunteers being in peril also.

Two months into the year, we received message tapes from our faraway children; heart ache messages. Philip had been engaged to Sue Wagstaff without ever telling us, and she had then gone to London. He had applied for entrance to Stockport College of Technology, with little or no prospects of getting back to Africa as a Wildlife Ranger. Communications were very difficult in those days, and then again, perhaps Philip had felt that his parents had gone off and done their own thing so may-be he should do the same. His brother Richard, aged 22 years old, had achieved a contract with the NHS to organise the feeding of all the patients and staff of the new Queen Elizabeth Hospital in Birmingham, whilst his wife Ann, the mine captain's daughter, was now a qualified teacher. They would all have preferred to be lounging by the pool in Ndola, with or without a job. Unfortunately Zambia now required immigrants to have a Work Permit. For that, academic qualifications or skilled experience was required. The Africans had a saying "The elephant does not give way to the rabbit."

Jo.

Jersey

2 country yokels got engaged in 1946

Richard left Zambia.

Birthday for Stecthford Hospital.

Phil became engaged.

Having spent much of our lives in the realms of Wild Africa and rural affairs in Tanzania with three children in tow, at our age of 46 years, we no longer needed canvas and camp cooking or protection from elephants and lions to do our job. However, we were still a rural oddity in need of soil augers, survey trainees, air photographs bull dozers and a drawing office for physical planning. I had learned how to protect myself from African chiefs and politicians and even witchcraft.

We were now living in quite a sophisticated urban environment when off duty, a modern world created by the previous Colonial Service administrators. We enjoyed a beautiful large furnished house and garden, numerous clubs with sporting facilities such as football, rugby, golf, sailing, swimming pools, tennis, flying, horse-riding, squash and 'shove-ha'penny' bars. I had joined the Photographic Society and made a few Kwacha creating black and white portraits of Ndola's beautiful ladies in my darkroom or should I say, with the help of my darkroom! I became a wedding photographer for my Swedish Volunteer Jiri Novak and his Swedish girlfriend.

We gently overcame our emotional desolation at the loss of our children with the help of weekend evenings out, dining and dancing with friends. We became totally overwhelmed by the seventies popular music from the U.K. and the U.S.A., created despite the horrors in Britain. Our house was teeming with visitors as a result of my chairmanship of the W.L.C.S.Z., but it was lovely to find so many new outdoor friends. Alan Heath showed us his collection of 3,000 Zambian tropical butterflies. He invited me to join him on his expeditions as he had heard that I used to collect moths on the farm in Norfolk. My two Rangers attended upon me each morning for instructions so we were now seriously apprehending poachers on road blocks, bringing in their ill-gotten gains to the prosperous Copperbelt marketplace, meat, skins, even baby animals for pets. Our two new Game Rangers needed paying and Jo exercised her charms on the Ndola Company Directors for funds with 100% success.

Norman Beaumont called me down to Lusaka to discuss the problem with our corrupt Bangladeshi and the resultant problems with my survey staff and the Swedish Volunteers. I met the Director of CUSO – Canadian University Overseas Service – who offered me Volunteers. I met also a lifelong Zambia/Malawi veteran of my discipline, land-use planning named Paddy Fleming. Here was a man who really understood the nature of the problems I faced and the skills that I had acquired. I was to hear from him again later. Norman thought the need to divert the Bangladeshi away from Rural Development to Agriculture was now imperative, but an element of racialism loomed. At my other meeting of the W.L.C.S.Z. Council, I met the famous 'lion man', Norman Carr from Luangwa Valley and arranged for him to come to us on 22nd March to help raise funds for paying my two Wildlife Rangers and Jo's Chongololo bus to take children to the education centre in Kafue National Park.

Here are a few names for posterity of our Ndola/Luanshya wild-lifers who worked hard in the cause at this time; Brian and Rita Jones, the Wagstaff family, Phillipe Deneux (a young Belgian world traveller, gemstone collector, glider pilot, photographer), Steve and Ila Bryant, Murray Denoon (an animal husbandry expert), the Tysons, Rod Emblem (a bird expert), Jean and Peter Ball, Alan Heath, Nigel and Christine Thomas, Martin Harvey.

Norman Carr told us that he had now released his two, now adult, lions in Kafue National Park with minimal success because being tame they tended to join the tourists at the Lodge Bar. So he then took them even further away; the Park is the size of France, and returned home to Luangwa Valley National Park without them. News came through later in the Press that two Dutch tourists had been scared out of their wits by two lions leaping on to their Land Rover bonnet and settling down for a sleep. Norman raised K384 that evening by telling his stories. He autographed my copy of his book "White Impala". Norman was well known worldwide from the film made about his life in Luangwa Valley where he lived alone with his two lions.

Baboons

At Jo's Trade Fair Zoo ground, the three baboons had escaped from their enclosure and were awaiting Jo's arrival at the entrance with enthusiasm for what they might achieve in their ascending status over their brother humans. As she stepped out of the car they dropped down upon her shoulders and pulled her hair to screaming point. She dropped her baskets, one of fruit and the other of cabbages which were immediately grabbed, plus unfortunately her car ignition keys, which was a clever trick, because that meant that their victim had no escape. They on the other hand, had a practiced escape route into the surrounding trees where they shouted with glee at Jo's tears.

Jo bombarded the baboons with large pieces of charcoal from the bag in her car boot creating a moment of insecurity amongst the villains which allowed the keys to be dropped. Jo apprehended the baboon as it dropped down to grab the keys and lobbed it into its cage. The final round-up took place with a furious waving of a long stick, creating the impression that life inside the enclosure was not so bad after all. On the way home there was a vehicle blockage at the traffic lights due to some driver being colour blind. The fire brigade were called and dozens of police. The latter became vociferous and banged on Jo's car roof, shouting orders to the accompaniment of sirens in the background. Jo said it was just like the zoo episode all over again, one policeman even tried to grab her keys!

Jo.

Charaxes spp.

Courtesy Alan Heath

Malawi Safari

We were always in raptures over our previous visit, such a beautiful and peaceful country, half of it being the tropical lake. Another chance arose with ten days leave due. Jack and Tommy Tyson expressed a desire to join us and offered a ride in their new Ford Cortina 2000. Hawker Siddley gave us a free overnight's stay at the Ridgeway Hotel in Lusaka en route. We enjoyed a dinner dance evening to be remembered. The next day we crossed the Luangwa River Bridge in the usual ritualistic style under the command of two armed youths of the Zambian Defence Forces. As we left they asked for cigarettes as a thank you for their security in crossing. Some would call it 'begging and bullying', a bit of an African habit which the Edwardians knew how to deal with and the Germans famously in Deutsch Ostafrika rather more positively with the Kiboko hippo hide whip. After hundreds of miles of uncultivated woodland we reached the Malawi border post.

We felt we were in a happier atmosphere after crossing the border, despite being told by officials that the ladies must cover their legs by Presidential Decree. The dirt road to capital Lilongwe was a nightmare as it was chewed up by Zambian lorries.

As dusk closed in, we encountered a khaki clad figure in the road. We thought at first he might be military so we slowed down but then realised that he held a spear in a threatening posture and wore a mask over his whole head. He was, believe it or not, a 'highwayman'. Could a man with a spear stop a car? Think of today's context of hijackers on jet airliners. Of course it works because a spear can break a windscreen and even kill a passenger. As it was, the figure was most frightening in appearance, being coated in khaki mud from head to toe and only a pair of short trousers with a fierce face peering through a mask.

Once it became obvious to the 'native' that we were submissive and stationary, he adopted the stance of a somewhat arrogant beggar, spear in one hand and one open outstretched palm. It was all a gimmick, albeit emotionally charged with uncertain consequences requiring some bravado on our part. The man stood beside the car window, his face now unmasked, seeking a reward. Jack ferreted in his pockets and produced a silver Zambian coin of no value in Malawi and tossed it to the ground. He childishly bent down to get it, thus giving us the chance to speed away. We did not report the matter to the Police Station in Lilongwe, fearing that we would be delayed with formalities, but mentioned it to the Chief Game Warden David Ansty, an old friend from Tanzania days, whom we had the pleasure of visiting en route to the lake.

Having feasted ourselves at Lilongwe Hotel, we set off on the morrow on a lovely but very narrow tar road towards Zomba. After some frightening experiences with stray sheep and goats (Zambian drivers don't have that hazard because the main roads are within state land, hence no villages), we reached Zomba.

Turning northwards towards the lake, we crossed a fertile plain with groups of dramatic mountains skirting the plain. The first group was called Dedza, very high into a cool wet climate and dense temperate rain forest. The plains were densely cultivated with crops and cattle, hence no food shortages as there was in Zambia.

We visited the old colonial town of Blantyre, lovely climate with a tea plantation nearby. The Tysons had no concept of agriculture and to drink tea from the surrounding plantation was a highlight of the holiday for them.

We had been recommended to visit Zomba plateau and stay at the Kachawa Inn. The approaching climb was so dramatic that we felt it was an achievement just to arrive. The African manager showed us our room. One side of this double bedroom was a wall of glass overlooking an escarpment with a view across the plains 3,000 ft below, an artist/photographer's dream. There was another side of Africa here, red soils, grassy rolling plains with scattered villages dotted with steep rocky hills, the scene changing colour in morning mists and evening blazing sunsets. Below us in miniature, was somewhat of a Gulliver Toyland's image created by the military barracks with a colourful military band and marching soldiers.

The view on the other side of the plateau was across the River Shire valley where elephants roamed and the Pied Crows wheeled and tumbled in acrobatic display rising and falling 2,000 feet on the thermals. In the mornings it was cold and misty at that altitude. The monkeys sat in the trees solemnly awaiting the sun's rays to set them aglow. In the evenings too we gathered around the log fire after playing darts with some local African dignitaries plus the Manager. The Manager was a very good player and having declared this to be a match, Blacks against Whites, he beat us hollow. That was an event we certainly could not enjoy in Zambia. I rather fancied getting a job in the Wildlife Department in Malawi. We were at an altitude of 6,000 ft with hot plains below. Some Europeans were lucky enough to live up on the forested plateau in the employ of the Forest Department. The high humidity and rainfall is the eco-climate for spectacular tree ferns, giant brambles, giant groundsel, and orchids.

It seemed that colonial influence took root earlier in Malawi than Zambia, the tree plantations on Zomba were mature and supported saw mills. There are also small dams stocked with Rainbow Trout. Jo and I wandered for miles and even climbed the peak with Tommy, which she did without complaint being of substantial physical proportions. Later, I did my usual sketching of birds for later identification whilst the others chatted.

We played Mahjong in the evenings by the fireside, a unique luxury compared to anywhere else in the East, West or Central Africa. We collected Mimosa seeds to plant in Ndola before setting off for warmer climes at the eastern end of the lake and an ancient town called Mangochi. What a place! Dry, dusty, great old spacious tin roof buildings, traffic (i.e. bicycles) galore, a ferry across the Shire River with a monument nearby, and cannon from a British gunboat dated 1899. These gunboats were to guard the local people from Arab slave traders. The gun was called a Hotchkiss Gun. The local museum introduced us to copies of rock paintings "from the stone age". These, remarkably, were a similar pattern to the ones we found on Petamikwa Hill in Miengwe. It appears that the lake had attracted human settlement for 100,000 years, finally attracting Arab businessmen collecting slaves. Dr David Livingstone initiated the death of the slave trade in the 1850's when the lake was called Nyasa.

"Jo, Dr Hastings Banda says you must cover your legs in Malawi."

Zomba Mountain

View over Zomba township

Nearby lay our ultimate destination Nkopola Lodge, a gorgeous site on the palm fringed shore of the glittering sky blue lake, the size of Wales.. Our bedroom overlooked the water and surprise, surprise there were ginger coloured fat-tailed sheep in the room enjoying the view. The little donkey on the veranda signified its dislike of Africans by bolting out of sight along the lake shore when his keeper came to tuck him up in his shed. The other Euro-friendly creature, sitting upon a rock near our balcony sunning itself and flicking its tongue to greet us, was a huge green monitor lizard, some five feet long. They eat fish so probably benefit from easy meals from the kitchen.

Catering was very good, fish meals predominated and we enjoyed chatting with guests about life in their home countries of South Africa, Malawi and Rhodesia. I found a canoe and better still a Proctor mini sailboard, like a super Dab-Chik, for me a kind of escape to tranquillity. One day the lake became shrouded in mist and standing on the shore was like being on the fringe of another world, the absolute silence, the sky and the water as one, grey. The spoken words of fishermen carried for miles revealing their secrets. Kayaking silently over great depths with zero visibility was an eerie experience for them. Then suddenly the silence was split by a pair of yodelling fish eagles, with an echo like being in a bathroom.

Sunbathing on the beach was not my scene. I had learned to treat the sun as public enemy number one, though the cheap Malawi Gin and orange juice afterwards, with 'the birds' certainly was not. The colourful feathered variety along the lake side 'bush' were also a magnet for me. I spent endless hours sketching them to later entertain the Wildlife Society Bird Group with a challenge to identify them. There are thousands of species of birds in Africa, as indeed there are of *Lepidoptera* and *Insectivore*, filling every nook and cranny of the habitat. According to DNA expert Adam Rutherford, there were originally thirteen species of *Homo* in and around African too.

Bedroom view

I loved the Dabchick on Lake Malawi

Nkopola Hotel on the lake

Nkapola Lodge. Tommy

Brian's obsession

Lake Malawi shore birds

.L.Malawi

Malawi

?
? ♀
1 – 10

Canary ?
flock in
fig tree

Flock Hawking for insects in the fig tree

Cisticola

Black Headed.

Black Headed Oriole.

8"

Wagtail
Common

Good songster

Nkpola Hotel
L, Malawi

162

Tropical Africa is the Garden of Eden, not the Middle East as depicted in the Bible. Apples don't grow there either. The prodigality of nature is greatest of all in Africa. In nature, there is no 'enough', just an immense extravagance, a golden shower of good things. Nature left to itself produces a myriad of everything. In Edwardian times when the breach loading rifle was invented, hunters came to Africa and found the continent from Cape Town northwards to the Sahara, absolutely teeming with elephants, threatening the survival of the hunters' wagon trains and their African porters. Even as recent as the 1950's, colonial times, Game Wardens were required to shoot 200 elephants per year – 'crop raiders' – or forfeit their pension rights.

During the ensuing days, Jo became happily conversational and entertaining with the Tysons and the other hotel guests in the relaxing lakeside atmosphere to the exclusion of me at times; my choice of course. My country girl soul-mate declared quietly, just before leaving Malawi for Zambia; "Brian, I need to stop trailing after you and develop my own interests now that our children have grown up and left us. You need to adjust."

I was a silent, glum passenger for many long hours en route for Lusaka. At the Ridgeway Hotel the Tysons were in their element meeting guests from their industrial background. Zambia, unlike Malawi, was and is today, an industrialised country. After dinner a dance band appeared, thankfully drowning the eternal boring small talk. Jo turned to me and said, "How about it then, lover boy."

And so the dark cloud lifted. Dancing was always a deeply emotional experience for us both from the age of 15 years old in the Leek Wootton Village Hut.

On the 27th November I found myself the local Returning Officer at Masaiti for the national Election; all very democratic despite being only one Party. The competition was between Candidates not Parties.

CHAPTER NINE

AUGUST 1975 - 1976

<u>8th August 1975</u>

Joshua E Chikoti was found dead in bed. His sudden death led to a post-mortem of which the result was "**Death from unknown causes**." Well now; I am very much aware of a deadly plant of the Genus *Datura* with gorgeous trumpet-shaped large white flowers known as Angel flowers which are often found on sale in garden centres in the U.K. The wild version is well known in Africa for its lethal toxicities, and in UK medical circles for its anaesthetic elements. These toxicities are untraceable by post-mortem. I am not saying that he was murdered of course, but I did detect a sigh of relief round the offices.

Chikoti-power emanated from modern education plus a handle on ancient customs, beliefs, and rituals, such that 20th century Europeans could not control or understand. The new African hierarchy were well aware of the machinations of witch doctors moving beyond the realms of modern education, viz., the Ndola C.I.D. had failed to pin down Chikoti for diverting government petrol into his own car, despite a legion of potential witnesses.

Having worked closely with Chikoti for many years, one might have assumed that I would be shocked and saddened; however, instead I felt happy that so many departmental staff could regain their working morale, and willingly pursue the national call to "rebuild the nation".

Joshua Chikoti was an intelligent African who had stepped boldly out of pre-Independent Northern Rhodesia, which terminated in October 1964. This region of Africa had suffered grievously under the influence of the racialist south and the Federation of Sir Roy Welensky, who was quoted as declaring, "I am determined to stop the tide of African nationalism."

Jo and |I had arrived in the third year of freedom from that regime, and the explosive morale change by year ten was quite remarkable. My African staff and colleagues were now educated and tuned into the modern world. They liked the British who had always been protective and had brought an element of prosperity for 'the common man'.

This breaking-out of an oppressive regime had been brought about by Kenneth Kaunda and his colleagues, supported prominently by;

1) Sir Steward Gore-Brown – a lifelong resident in Northern Province,
2) Sir John Moffat, born in Rhodesia of a distinguished missionary family. He had strived for "Early Independence, and not have to wait for the majority of Africans to become literate."

3) Sir Ronald Prain, Chairman of R.S.T. mining company. He responded with a practical view; "…. must be faced squarely and dealt with realistically if changes are to take place in an orderly manner."

One link with the past that was decidedly not broken was beer drinking. The traditional African villager consumption was limited by the women's capacity to ferment enough 'chibuku' whereas there were in the mine townships Beer Halls, with the consumption limited only by the amount of kwacha in the mineworker's pockets. In the mine beer halls only branded beer was allowed to be sold and no spirits or wine. Bottled beer was also available all along the road to Lusaka, so it was every-man-for-himself as to who could get to Lusaka first without running off the tarmac.

August 1975
Life had changed for us; it was seven years since we were in Mombasa getting our daughter Caroline married off to Iain. Our two boys at the time had enjoyed the coastal palm-fringed coral beaches and the Tsavo National Park nearby. We were now bereft of our children. Caroline now lived ostentatiously in Tokyo, Richard was married and struggling in poverty stricken Britain and Philip was gambling with life's challenges amongst the 'Satanic Mills' instead of being a Wildlife Ranger in Zambia as had been his ambition. In fact it was as well, since Philip was a hungry soul, over six feet tall and Zambia was progressing towards starvation, unable to import food with the copper price on the floor and the southern border closed.
We decided to indulge in a weekend at Kashiba Lake. There was now a government Rest House there with a servant/cook to heat water for the bath! We enjoyed curried chicken and coffee to the sound of crickets under a new moon in the window. Sitting on the veranda afterwards, to the sound of a hissing Tilley lamp and the occasional cries of nightjars, we became stormed by large furry mole crickets, striking the lamp at high speed. The very bright light attracted nightlife including mosquitoes and other undesirables. We discovered mole crickets to our dismay, crawling over the floor to join us in the bedroom.
John Koni, the old *madala,* was striking up the bathroom fire. It took him about two hours before he shouted, "Mukwai, bafu is ready." Hence we enjoyed a honeymoon style shared large *bafu* in the light of the hissing Tilley lamp, to the accompaniment of mole cricket chirps. Mutual attentiveness was invoked in the excitement of a wild place and microwave messages fleeted silently between us, persons and minds without words. "Brian, tell that madala we don't need him until tomorrow." It was, for me, one of those situations when mankind needs a beautiful wife,

unfettered by anxieties, unclothed, uninhibited, unashamed, and unrepentant, in the vastness of Ndola Rural District.

Back in Ndola, Monday morning was one of those days unlike that at Lake Kashiba, that started off badly. Di Bushel my Wildlife Society Secretary, phoned croaking and swearing about what had not been done whilst she was away on holiday. Jo answered and faced an onslaught, but she held her temper. We loaded our car with food and escaped for a few days at Miengwe Scheme prior to Jo's new PNEU Prep-School starting. We were expecting the artist David Shepherd shortly and needed to organise a social event in the Lowenthal Theatre in town with films, his paintings, posters and refreshments; tickets to be 5 kwacha (£2.50). "Over to you Di!"

Trees along the road into Miengwe were now showing their spring colour in anticipation of rain; the red *Brachystegia spp.* yellow *Mupundu* orange *Albizia sp.* and the evergreen *Syzigium sp.* with its fragrant white blossom. Miengwe was a piece of 'Dry Upland Forest' in an enclave of otherwise *Miombo Woodland* area that covers the vast northern half of Zambia. Hence Miengwe was free of the Tsetse fly associated with *miombo*, which is death to cattle and horses and to humans where sleeping sickness prevails. The Peugeot went well except that when the garage vetted the car they managed to fill 'the hooter' with water so that when a duiker antelope appeared in the road, we could only muster a faint gurgle.

Miombo Woodland   *Spring colours.*

Woodland 'Rhodesian

Miengwe borehole water supply.

In Miengwe I was annoyed to find local pyromaniacs burning the windows of trees cleared by my bulldozers instead of making charcoal and selling it to the mines for their smelters. Aminoff arrived from Lusaka with his new girlfriend Anna and two black girls aged about eighteen. My shoulder was paining me and Jiri Novak said, "Right Brian, I'll get the sauna going – that'll fix it."

We could not persuade the giggling black girls to join us in the sauna, in fact we never did get an African into the sauna even though they were quite happy to bathe naked in the contour dam – the teenagers that is. The two girls commandeered Jiri's bed, leaving him to sleep in the sauna, whilst we were in the caravan. We didn't see them at breakfast with Frederik Aminoff, Anna, Jiri Novak and us. So they proved to be two not very sociable town girls.

Frederik was obviously planning to marry Anna; hence the topic of marital success arose. He planned to break away from Sweden and go for a better life in Rhodesia as a farmer "in the best climate in the world," he said. At this time Rhodesia was still a prosperous, well educated, multi-racial country with valuable export crops of Virginia tobacco and maize. It was a feature of the line-of-rail from Salisbury, now Harare, through Zambia to the Copperbelt and on to Angola, to see mountains of maize bags from Rhodesia beside the track awaiting distribution.

Jo declared about marital bliss, "If one partner says anything that tends to reflect criticism upon the other's intelligence or wisdom, or their looks or hygiene, then that arouses immediate and unwarrantably extreme reaction. This kind of thing can lead to a dislike of the other person. Don't you agree, Brian?"

"Yes of course. Can't avoid accidental criticism some times though. Stick with good manners, and always be polite with the opposite sex, that's what I learnt at my boys' only secondary school. Never argue with a woman, **they are always right**, evolution made them that way simply because they have to raise the next generation to be better than the last one. Starved of the female side of life at school, we boys finished our education worshipping the opposite sex and would never criticise any female; to her face."

Rhodesian maize arr[...] in Zambia. Pre-Independence.

No tractors at Miengwe - yet

Vegetables for Ndola market

Petamikwa Hill at Miengwe

Back at home we frequently saw KK cutting down a tree on T.V. whenever a ceremonial event occurred. It is interesting that the opposite occurs in the U.K. The Queen always plants a tree. When we climbed Petamikwa Hill, we would gaze northwards upon the endless forest stretching for thousands of square miles to the Tanzania border. No wonder cutting down trees is viewed as the road to future prosperity in Zambia.

3rd October 1975 – David Shepherd Day.

The famous artist and conservationist was born in 1931 and sadly died in 2017 leaving behind him the David Shepherd Wildlife Foundation which provides finance for Zambia's Chongololo Programme, reaching all primary schools with wildlife education material. He was our guest on this occasion, staying with us for the several days of our programme of films, exhibitions of his paintings and social gatherings throughout the Copperbelt towns and cities.

Di Bushell collected him from the airport, a thrilling experience for her and a dynamic one for him. We had no idea what sort of personality he was, but we arranged for Jo to take him out to lunch with Nancy Wagstaff and a swim in her pool. It was extremely hot, suicide-month, and he was bound to be in need of refreshment after his long journey. It turned out that he was the most unostentatious person one could ever hope to meet, especially in view of his fame. Jo, Nancy Wagstaff and David Shepherd proved to be three vivacious people, full of humour and fun. Jo later told me that Friday had been one of the happiest days of her life; I should mention that I was attending the Provincial Development Committee. Di expressed amazement at how Jo and David were on the same wavelength within fifteen seconds of meeting and she said, "You are old friends then?"

360 people turned up for his presentation of the BBC film about his life with steam trains, "*Last Train to Mulobezi*". He was happy watching it for the umpteenth time. As a personality he was outspoken and quite blunt about people and situations he did not approve of in relation to conservation of wildlife, especially elephants. I had on my wall at home an elephant print, I think his first, with Kilimanjaro in the background, which I picked up years ago in Dar es Salaam, Tanzania, for thirty shillings. David admiringly declared "When I am dead, that picture will make a fortune." In fact we sold it when we were leaving Zambia in 1977, in aid of the Conservation Society, for £650.

For all David's 'self-culture' which he declared was "a must if you need to make money", he was on our shortlist of people we loved. He was one of the few people who instantly and intensely observed the creative nature of us, and our children. We showed him photos of our faraway children and an oil painting of Caroline entitled, "She's beautiful." "What lovely shiny blonde hair," he said. He thought Richard's O-Level paintings were "a much higher standard than mine at that age."

<u>Late 1975 News</u>

1) We made a profit of kwacha 900 on the D.S. Lowenthal Theatre evening.
2) USA have finally pulled out of Vietnam after their defeat by the Viet Cong. Their legacy; 25 million bomb craters and millions of acres of rainforest destroyed by "agent orange", presumably 245 T, a hormone brush-wood killer?
3) The total cost of food imports to Zambia in 1974 was 45 million kwacha, all of which food could be produced in Zambia. I guess that's why we were there.
4) Israel and Egypt were trying to make peace, initiated by Henry Kissinger of USA.
5) President Ford of USA narrowly escaped assassination by a 40 year old woman. The trouble was they could buy firearms at the 'corner store' which prevented second thoughts setting in.
6) Civil War was raging in Angola now the Portuguese colonisers had left. Arms were being supplied by communist Cuba. We had refugees in western Zambia.

Kafue National Park

Towards the end of the year we were invited to Kafue National Park by the Game Department. There was a plan to set up an Education Centre for African school children. Jo hoped to use this idea but we would need to raise money to buy a mini bus in due course.

North Kafue N.P.
Education Centre

Photo by Robert Taylor

Kafwala camp Kafue Nat., Park   Philip,Richard,June,Ann,Jo,Brian,Robert Taylor

1971

Kafue River

Lechwe in Bangweulu swamps.

Courtesy Ian Tanner, WLCSZ.

Saddle-billed stork.

177

We reached Kafwala tourist camp. There were four servants, the only humans in the 22,400 square kilometres of park, the senior one being Jackson. Jackson had been there nine years and thrived on fish from the mighty Kafue River flowing past the door when the refrigerated stock of food ran out. The river was such a noisy place, at all levels of the biosphere immense activity, even at the hottest time of day the creatures were "at it", wooing, hunting, hiding, singing, wallowing, travelling, establishing their territorial rights.

The river teamed with life, not to mention the hippos that graze the banks at night and deposit their surplus to requirement next day to fertilize the river. The river after boiling tasted really pleasant, especially the coffee, we wished we could take some back to Ndola. However we view the wildlife, the natural world, albeit a source of wonder for the human race today as of peace and relaxation, it is not so however for the participants on this stage. For the performers it is a matter of survival, a struggle to defeat the driver of evolution; **death.** The creatures enjoy freedom here but this is not their haven of peace.

Death everywhere.

We were intrigued by a number of events at Kafwala;

a) Jackson's finesse in the kitchen with his old wood stove and his skill at catching small mouth bream with small crabs.

b) The beautiful view from the shady cool of the *sitenge,* a grass thatched *banda* where we ate, enjoying the wafting clean fresh river air, a welcome escape from the sultry sodden heat of the upland bush.

c) The myriad of species of colourful birds each with their own mating calls for the start of the rainy season.

d) The blazing inferno raging in the uplands of the Park. Jackson said he had never seen such an inferno in his nine years in the Park. The fire burnt every part, both sides of the fire-brake roads, leaving a landscape of charcoal to sustain the animals. Obviously fires do not start by a freak of nature, so who started this and why?

e) The big boys of the river, very noisy and pugnacious. The event detailed in the Visitors Book whereby some African Rangers and three children aged 8-10 years old, were over turned in their boat by the hippos. One African and the white children could swim and reached an island in the river. The two African Rangers were never found, probably devoured by crocodiles. Many hours passed before their cries were heard. A long trek to another Ranger Camp called Chunga, resulted in; no boat. Returning to Kafwala at 9.00 pm, a radio call was achieved to Treetops, on the river flats reserve many hours away. They arrived with a canoe at 11.00 pm. A call was made for volunteers to take to the river in the blackness of night but they were hard to come by; so the record stated. They were rescued eventually.

f) Three mighty buffalo bulls, against the charcoal black background appeared and scared us to death. They were followed by a cloud of Tsetse flies which set-to to drink our blood;

g) The Darters seemed to swim underwater with just their heads above water. No wonder they had to hang out their wings to dry. Nature fills every gap in the environment.

Buffalo in huge mumbers.

Baboons

Elephant Jamboree

By Katelyn Williams

Sable

KAFUBU STATE DAIRY

No sooner back from our trip than we found HQ dignitaries on our doorstep wanting to review the Israeli projects' situation. From Kafulafuta we trundled off to see our new State Dairy just outside Luanshya, and to greet the President Dr Kenneth Kaunda there. We were all impressed with the work of the Italian Manager. The land I had cleared with Paddy Prendergast was now plush green with Kikuyu grass, and three bulls were out on display. In the rainy season the farming system was to make silage to carry the cattle over the next dry season. The silage clamp was a patent design of mine from my Norfolk farming days; built of wood from the woodlands we had cleared with my bulldozers. The Manager had built it impressively. "Where has this design come from?" enquired the President.

"Come and look at the Milking Parlour," responded Piero, not wishing to distract focus from his management achievements. I took photographs for the Press.

Piero Augustinelli with President Kaunda **Kafubu State Dairy**

182

We planted Kikuyu grass

Kafubu State Dairy

183

Silage clamp.

Milking parlour Luanshya dairy

Schoolboys at Kafubu Dairy

"The lawn needs mowing Brian"
Too much to do in 1975.

CHAPTER TEN

1976

With the International Money Fund having now taken over the U.K. economy sterling was falling fast. Jo and I switched our U.K. savings account into U.S. dollars. Meantime, I received a letter from Richard in Birmingham saying that he was planning to set themselves up with a car of a make recommended by "good old Dad" a Peugeot, and could I possibly lend him £700. Actually, I considered our savings would hold its value better in a car than in a bank account. The Arabs had a related idea, "They are buying up London", Richard said. In the meantime Zambia had devalued the kwacha by 20%, which meant that our cost of living had shot up, living as we did very much on imports.

1st January 1976

We had made a decision, to find somewhere to live when my contract ended the following year. Visitors were telling us, "When you retire, whatever you do don't go back to UK, everyone's leaving". Hence the property market was falling dramatically. We decided that now was the time for Jo to go to England, see all the children and look for a house. Her plane was 5.30 pm and we enjoyed a champagne and good wishes departure with some friends, the Wagstaffs, Jiri Novak, Tysons, Ila and Steve Bryant, Liz and Derek Smith who were going to keep the school going, Wisharts, Eileen O'Dell the farmer who helped feed our animals. So that was all very jolly and Jo blew me a kiss from the departing plane step. She looked such an attractive figure crossing the apron in white trousers and a pale green flimsy blouse under the bright sunny blue sky. It was to be a shock when her comfortable VC10 touched down at Gatwick in the freezing darkness!

My silent house seemed barren, not simply empty. I hurriedly left and went to see Ewe Gerstel about arranging a film night over a noggin of whiskey, which carried me sulkily until 8.30 pm and home to an early, haunted bed. I set the alarm for 5.45 am and off I went to Miengwe to see how our Swedish volunteers were getting on in that now well-established resettlement scheme. The day following was to be our Film Festival at the Lowenthal Theatre dedicated to fundraising. It was always well attended. I would thenceforth be kept busy with Society affairs, organising my two Game Rangers, and the ten agricultural projects under my umbrella. The Copperbelt State Cabinet Minister had offered me an office in his Building! I was to be the only white face in a hundred staff, although I never noticed it. *"Maybe I am half African after all these years?"*

I received letters from Jo in the U.K. who was now enjoying life with the family including Caroline and her husband Iain who had left Japan and were resident in England awaiting a Green Card to enter the U.S.A. Iain had a job offer in Seattle in Washington State. Jo had three problems; the weather was freezing, our son Philip's life was falling apart due to Sue Wagstaff breaking off their engagement, and the children wanted her to extend her stay until mid-February. She didn't take much persuading. I hoped that such a long separation would never happen again, the emotional strain of being separated from one's progeny and soul-mate was unnatural. She told me that they were all together in Richard and Ann's house in Stechford, Birmingham drinking Richard's homemade wine and toasting Dad. This missing Dad was a recurrent topic in conversation I was told, as they had only ever known Mum and Dad as very much 'one-being'.

The problem with the weather was very real for Jo whose bones ached with cold she said, also that she and Caroline had to sleep together in the same bed to survive. "The windows are iced up on the inside in the morning". When I thought of her sunbathing in tropical heat by the swimming pool only three days before, I became quite concerned for her health. The main topic of conversation she said was life at Home Farm in Norfolk. She expressed amazement at their detailed memory of every small daily detail of their lives as children on the farm. I think that phase in their lives made them who they are today. They also dreamed of Africa. They decided to visit Twycross Zoo in mid-January and stroked the giraffe, which seemed to favour Richard for some reason, but then it was always his school boy ambition to be a vet. Jo said that Richard's wine was so strong that they went to bed sozzled in order not to notice the cold bedroom! Jo later travelled all over Southern England, including visiting my sister Joy who took her to London to see the show Black Mikado with which she was absolutely enthralled; perhaps it reminded her of Zambia? After visiting East Sussex and her 12 cousins there, she drove to Budleigh Salterton in East Devon where Ila and Steve Bryant's builder father lived and might help us find a place in that gorgeous seaside town. Her efforts to find a house did not bear fruit but she had set her heart on the New Forest which was wild like Africa.

Back in Zambia the President declared a National Emergency. I was getting worried that Jo and I had no bolthole to go to. It was mainly food shortages with the border to the south firmly closed, but some other factors too, for example Zambia's support for the anti-Communist army in Angola, which was the losing side against Cuban support for the rebels. This had led the Angolan port of Lolito Bay to be closed to Zambia. This important copper export outlet was served by the railway from Ndola. Unfortunately, our only other outlet Dar es Salaam in Tanzania was suffering from "congestion". The Chinese Tan-Zam Railway was near completion.

I had a growing problem with feeding the two baboons at the Trade Fair Zoo and decided to undertake an exercise in 'returning them to the wild'. It proved to be another troublesome exercise; baboons are not as stupid as they look and they had a preference for the easy life in the zoo as opposed to foraging for morsels in the bush. I must say that I felt sympathetic, being somewhat deprived myself at the time,

30th January 1976
"Dearest Jo.

The time is 10.30 pm. Where have I been all this time? Well, Miengwe yet again! I still have three Caterpillar D7 bulldozers around my neck, also two bottles of water. Thereby lays a story: Your employee Noel Badrian came with me to help with the two baboons which were in a box on the roof rack. We released them (or tried to) on the west side of Balnabeen Hill. It was raining and they preferred the box. We drove them off with stones, like the stoning of erring women in biblical Jerusalem. I also tried the sudden opening of my umbrella trick which I used to frighten the lions down that survey trace in Tanzania, but they would have none of it and came back to the footpath by my car. A slow moving train came along and they obviously had it in mind to jump on board for Ndola. We waved our arms frantically.

Eventually they found a bush of sweet apricot like fruits, *Uapacca sp.*, which I also tasted and tucked into. Noel took a photograph of us enjoying our lunch break. One came up to me with his arms outstretched in a thank you gesture of affection. I shooed him off and he climbed five feet up a tree and jumped across to the fruit tree, slipped and feel and twisted his neck. He was just not used to climbing these types of trees. As to climbing Balnaabeen Hill nearby, where they are supposed to take refuge from their enemies, well, I really think they will die of exhaustion if they ever reach the top. Anyhow, they came back to their box and we had to snatch it away. Then very heavy rain necessitated us using rain capes and my umbrella. After five minutes, we had two baboons cuddling up under the umbrella. We decided to run away and hide. We hoped they would learn some fear of being alone.

Finally, we drove off, or I should say ploughed, towards the main road in the car, through mud and water and hit a stump which removed my exhaust pipe! We were now popping along like a motor boat. The rain was torrential. It did not deter the policemen on the main Ndola road block. They had hand guns, it was like being in the U.S.A. They asked to examine the box. On the way out, we had told them that we had baboons, whereupon the armed braves recoiled in fright. On the return, I told the policemen that we had let the baboons go because they were hungry. They asked where they were and I told them that they were on the train back to Ndola. The police said that that was good news because there was a police checkpoint on the railway station in Ndola and if they were not carrying their registration cards, they would definitely be apprehended. I adopted a confident manner and told them that the baboons were fully paid up members of both U.N.I.P. and the W.L.C.S.Z. Laughter all round and we departed in good spirits!

Lots of love, Brian X"

The Swedish community invited me to their party at the Chinese Restaurant. There was a full-blown dinner and then wild dancing. Jiri Novak had obviously told them that I was alone and emotionally desperate for company because two women in particular set about driving me mad on the dance floor. They were very practiced in arousal techniques. The following day I saw a film called "Girls are for Loving" with nude scenes every five minutes. I should not have gone! I was advised by my good friends Steve and Ila Bryant that I was a "glutton for punishment"! .

Eagle Travel in Ndola told me that 200 people were leaving with one-way tickets, every week. Jo and I were determined to persevere until the end of my contract in two years' time. Frederick Aminoff, my Swedish volunteer manager, was also off to Rhodesia, leaving Jiri Novak in charge for now. I asked Jiri how he could afford to buy his new Fiat 127 car. Hence the amazing story of how Jiri escaped to Sweden from Russian occupied Czechoslovakia in 1968. He fled with a bag given to him by his mother, containing one kilogram of antique gold coins. He sold those to a Jew in Vienna for US$40,000. When Jiri was 18 years old, he was interrogated by armed police in a dark cell and forced to sign documents. These apparently handed over his father's estates to the Government. His mother escaped to their villa in the mountains. His grandfather was imprisoned for criticising the Communist Party at the age of 71 years. He later died. Jiri later saw one of his father's paintings in an Art Gallery. The Curator said that they had paid US$ 144,000 for it. No-one knew who pocketed that money. Jiri said, "In Czechoslovakia if you are out of a job, you are sent to the mines as slave labour. My country has always been walked-over. In 1820 the Swedes plundered all its wealth, and then subsequently the country was conquered by the Hapsburg Empire of Austria and latterly by the Germans. There has always been an Upper Class of landowners with castles in Czechoslakia."

My diary states: Jiri ended up with a sore throat and went to our doctor, Dr Mac Nab. Donald gave him an 'equine' dose of some German medicine which floored him for a couple of hours. I went to Eagle Travel to see if Jo's name was on any of the flight lists for the next two weeks but nothing. I took three prizes for colour slides from Malawi at the Photo Society. The price of mealie meal doubled.

I wrote to Jo and told her that I needed a transfusion of her love to overcome my longing. My hydraulics was decidedly low! In the meantime, a letter arrived on my desk in the Cabinet Office from the Prime Minster no less, telling me to compile the Third National Development Plan for the Copperbelt Province. I reckoned that would take me two years. He went on to say that he would like a plan for 100 dams for irrigating farmlands of small farmers "by next Tuesday". That took my mind off Jo. I was in need of that play at Lowethal Theatre that I had booked for an evening with the Bryants, entitled "Come Back into my World." It was a very humorous play fortunately.

12th February 1976

Jo arrived four hours late. One would have thought that our meeting would have been rapturously over-whelming with joy and happiness. We just felt like that but didn't show it. To the casual airport entrance lounge observer, we were man and wife warmly welcoming each other with reserve, in public. "Hello Jo. Good flight?"

"Yes Brian, it went very well. I am glad to get back into the warm. How are you?"

"There's something wrong with my body machine. I have been in agony all day."

"Oh dear. Is it my fault, for arriving late?"

Sadly I had developed a severe abdominal pain plus diarrhoea and had finally collapsed into my bed under the supervision of Dr Donald Mac Nab. Tests were sent off and returned by 24th February by which time I had lost six pounds in weight. A later diagnosis revealed that I had been born a Coeliac and my condition had resulted from an inferior diet of too much bread, my kitchen supervisor having swanned off to the U.K.! Jo now put me back on mealie meal – maize meal – the staple diet of all Zambians, and I recovered.

Jo was saying about UK, "I don't know why you lumber your Uncle Tom up with all those old letters and diaries of yours Brian?"

"Writing diaries is a habit. It began when I was a Boy Scout. I found a diary from my student days about a girl that I spent the weekend with. It was a fly-fishing weekend with three fellow students in a tiny Inn called the Packhouse Inn in Dovedale. I hit it off with this girl because she had met with tragic circumstances in Nazi Holland which matched my own circumstances in the Blitz on Coventry, thus giving us a topic to chat about, and make friends, courtesy of Adolf of ill-repute. She was the same age as me and we had a riotous sing-song evening with my ukulele and my student pals. I remember being hugely attracted by her large dark-eyes and bushy black eye-brows. She told me she was a dancer. I looked her up in the Visitors Book when we were leaving, her name was Audrey Hepburn."

At the theatre Jo and I found it full of white faces but not familiar ones, some other nationalities still arriving in Zambia it seemed. We spoke to some old stalwarts who declared to us that they were definitely not leaving; surnames, Balls, Bish, Leggatt, Rioch, Toft, Dell, Storrs.

18th March 1976

Jo's school children were doing very well on the PNEU system faced as they were with passing entrance exams for private sector secondary boarding schools overseas. The PNEU – Parents National Education Union – system was an education course sponsored by the UK. Foreign Office for families posted overseas. It proved to be a very high standard but requiring text books from the U.K. Two of Jo's pupils were Dutch with only a smattering of English words which was quite a challenge; they ended up top of the class.

Our Bank Manager neighbour was heard to say over-the-fence but within earshot, "She thinks she's Queen of the Universe that woman, with her Chongololo campaign for all Primary Schools, the Zoo, driving about with a cheetah on the back seat, and chatting up famous people like David Shepherd and KK." That was not a description of Jo's character at all; Jo was born a humble person of 'commoner' village ancestry. She did not suffer from ulterior motives, she just suffered from un-bounding energy, both mental and physical, thus making her presence felt where minds were at work, any minds; politicians, scientists, theatre-folk, bank managers and where minds were not at work and should be, like Miengwe village women, house servants and school children. Jo was youthful in her forties and a fireball for the opposite sex to trifle with, in view of that fiery gene that she had inherited from her father Arthur Marriott.

Audrey.

Jo's kindergarten schoolchildren.

Thinking ....monkey business.

Arthur Marriott was a laugh a minute clown, which endowed his daughter with a desire to make people laugh 'straight off the cuff' when meeting even complete strangers, from the Vice President to the Miengwe village women, who could not speak a word of English, or greeting the visitors to the Zoo in Trade Fair Week with a Sykes Blue Monkey sitting on her shoulder. I enjoyed many long hours chatting with Sergeant Marriott of the Royal Horse Artillery in WWI. He absolutely loved horses, his ambition as a boy was to become a jockey. He knew I was heading towards a farming career and he made me swear to keep draught horses on my farm as a condition of him giving his daughter's hand to me in marriage. In those days a father had to give consent if his daughter was under the age of twenty one.

We loved to 'get away from it all' whenever we could and go on safari in the vast southern region of the Ndola Rural District, going further south to the Lukanga Swamps through Chief Mwinuna's unpopulated area, or to squat on a limestone rock overlooking the intensely clear blue depths of Kashiba Lake, wearing as little as possible, like we did in the remote Ngualla volcano crater lake in Southern Tanzania. We imbibed the immensity of nature's creativity in these places that had been the realm of *Loxodonta africana* in their multi-thousands for past 20 million years or so, as compared to the promiscuous *Homo spp.* for only one and a half million years. It was no surprise that Africans had a complex; feeling small. Africans have now adopted from Europeans the technique of showing largeness and power by for example, wearing a pin-striped suit in the office and sporting a chair, unknown in the traditional villages, or driving a big lorry or a bulldozer, or wearing a cowboy hat, or sporting an AK47.

Jo skinny dipping in Ngualla volcano crater

On safari in Zambia

Kafue River supermarket

Mwinuna, Zambia, 1970

We managed to show two wonderful films at Lowenthal Theatre to raise funds at kwacha 2 per ticket. These were called "African Elephant" and "The Crowded Valley". The theatre was packed and at last we persuaded our dear friend Nancy Wagstaff's reluctant husband to bring her, and she absolutely loved it all, even more than her pet rabbit that had the free run of her house. The films were then shown in Luanshya Mine Township by our new Society Members Pam Green, Dina Jones and Dick Downing with huge success, ending with them enrolling scores of new members and collecting one-thousand-kwacha cash.

The Wagstaffs soon left Zambia along with general rush to escape famine. Their children having become adults, they took a job in Southern Sudan with the World Bank, Ivan was an accountant, on an agricultural development project. Sadly, Nancy was bitten by a mosquito that was a vector of contagious meningitis carried by some pigs there and quickly died. We were devastated.

Jo and I felt very much a part of the campaign to boot up food production and indeed to boot up wildlife conservation education. We were going to be very busy indeed for the remaining year of my contract. My two Wildlife Rangers were holding road blocks with Police backing occasionally. The Evidence to Court, animal meat, tended to disappear before the case came up, there were no freezers available. We also had our free-range rabbits running in the garden plus two geese, two Muscovy ducks and my .22 calibre rifle for the occasional safari guinea fowl. Our poultry farmer friend, Mrs O'Dell kept us supplied with eggs and poultry meat.

July 1976 – The first plot of wheat grown in Northern Zambia
It was time to impress some distinguished guests as to how practical it might be to grow wheat in Copperbelt Province as a back-up to copper. My guests were, Mr Guy Scott was an agricultural advisor to the Zambian Government and a distinguished commercial farmer in the south, Mr A N Beaumont was the Director of Rural Development in the Civil Service, Dr Peter Heilmann was a soil scientist from my office, Mr Pressguard from the Norwegian Aid Agency, and a representative of the Zambia Times newspaper. Wheat is a northern climate crop, hence when grown in the cooler dry season it has to be irrigated.

My D7 Caterpillar bulldozer had made a straight track down to Lake Inampamba for about three miles and the plot looked magnificent, irrigated by water from the lake. Mr Scott stepped up the pump to full pressure to see if the lake level would drop after half an hour. It did not. It was acclaimed as a "Stepping stone to attracting a major company and

197

eventually contributing to resolving the food shortage." [This was previously reported upon in this book.]

<u>August 1976</u>
My hunting instincts emerged again when we had befriended Alan Heath whom, albeit an employee of the mining corporation RCM, had become over-whelmed by his scientific nature and was now heading towards becoming a full blown Lepidopterist. I joined him in the hunt through the forests for the dramatically beautiful Charaxes species. His room at home was a museum of perfectly preserved and labelled specimens. His two children had become avid collectors also. Wife Pauline however, felt that she would need to sprout colourful wings if she was going to continue a close and happy relationship with Alan. In the outcome, at the end of his contract, Alan followed the abundance of butterflies to Rhodesia whilst Pauline escaped to England. Alan managed to get himself apprehended by soldiers patrolling the Congo Border beyond Mufulira Ranch on one occasion. They did not believe his explanation as to his activities and declared him a spy.

Bearded wheat trial, irrigated, Inampamba Lake.

Lakeside bearded wheat trial

Hybrid maize trial Munkumpu

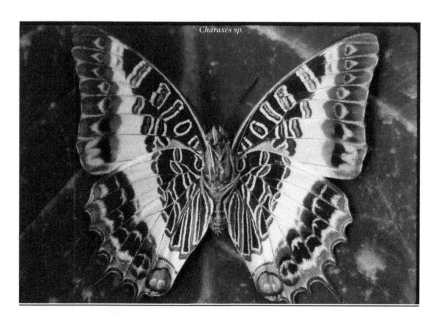

Charaxes sp.

<u>September 1976. Extracts from my monthly Members Newsletter :</u>
Report on a three-day road block on a popular exit road for poachers.
Participants:- E Woodhouse, A Lukuwa, G Mushitu (our game guards) six Government Game Guards from Chilanga, Police Officers and me.
Two road blocks were set up and five people arrested;

1) A Mufulira, Copperbelt man was charged with offences for "a) failing to endorse his National Game Licence and b) being in possession of government trophies without a licence for one Tesebe, four Reedbuck, and three Common Duiker.
2) An Mpika man from Northern Province with five elephant tusks without a licence,
3) A Kabilushi, Copperbelt woman for being in possession of one Reedbuck and one Duiker without a licence,
4) An Ndola man was charged with having one Common Duiker without a licence
5) An Ndola man was charged with being in possession of a Common Duiker and a Reedbuck without a licence."

Report on the weight of the Law: "A Luanshya Copperbelt man was arrested on 24th July at a road block and was found in possession of six Common Duiker and two Reedbuck without licences. At Ndola Magistrates Court on 26th August, Mr Kiddy Caishala was fined 1,000 kwacha or nine months hard labour in default."

Such heavy sentences can only encourage the anti-poaching patrols and the Game Rangers in their dedicated and selfless work. However, it must be said that some magistrates in this country are still imposing quite trivial sentences that bear no relation either to the commercial/illegal value of the goods confiscated or the new Ministry enthusiasm and striving to stem the tide of poaching that is threatening Zambia's wildlife resources.

24th-30th October 1976

We climbed into Alan Heath's station wagon and took the 'back way' to Northern Malawi's Nyika Plateau National Park instead of trekking down to Lusaka. This was a much shorter route. It was mainly unpopulated wild 'bush' after a stopover at the White Father's Mission at Isoka in the Northern Province. Only two Fathers' remained in that large building; John was from the Welsh mountains, a young school teacher whose pay of 25 ngwee per day (about £0.12), necessitated a chicken farm for eggs and broilers, the profits from which were earmarked for the Bishop at Kasama. The chicken feed had to be hauled in from far away Lusaka in the South, so profits were not a strong feature of the exercise We drove eastwards in Mayombe District towards the border which necessitated a climb up to 7,000 feet altitude via an escarpment track. We found ourselves in rolling grassland, park-like, unspoilt by tourists, but seemingly the preserve of a few expatriate Malawian residents of the Park authorities and who kept quiet about their mini-paradise. A Senior Ranger with the illustrious name of Major Gordon looked after the place, servicing four chalets (log cabins) and collecting licences for fishing in the well-stocked trout lake.

We felt like the landed gentry 'of yore' in England, with servants and a view from our front door of wild and beautiful parklands rolling away into the distance where we could stroll and admire the beds of *Moraea* Irises and the carpets of purple Ground Orchids. The climate was perfect for us five humans, with 25 degrees centigrade with a fresh breeze in the daytime and cold evenings by a log fire. The herds of Roan Antelope sprinkled the landscape like Fallow Deer in the parklands in England, but not much else. We drove around at night with headlights and spotted a leopard lurking in a valley bottom. A very different place to the lowland parks in Zambia, teeming with noisy wild creatures. Our overall costs for the one-week holiday turned out to be only K170 (£85).

Alan and Pauline Heath and ? on the Nyika. *Martin Elbourne*

Nyika Plateau Malawi
7000 ft.   21

Impression of Nyika Plateau

Diary copy

Nyika Plateau 7000 ft

Nyika 7000 ft

The Tan Zam Railway was finally declared open at the end of the year. There was great rejoicing that Zambia could now market its copper bars via Dar es Salaam in Tanzania and we could drive away the Somali ivory traders, not to mention the 22,000 Chinese "engineers" who frequently visited Ndola with shopping trollies creating periodic famine. They compensated by buying bales of tobacco from local farmers, much to the chagrin of the Tobacco Board of Zambia.

The new African Provincial Agricultural Officer restored my drawing office and staff vehicles to their original buoyant state, including the welcome addition of a young lady from England who was a Geography graduate to assist me with the survey of Mpongwe Development Zone for the purpose of government documentation of the new boundary of State Land. Her name was Elizabeth Smith, a hardy soul facing an enormous challenge having to live under canvas along the boundary in uninhabited remote locations and with only my junior African surveyors for company. She was shepherded by Jo when she was in town and she helped with Jo's new project, Chongololo.

A V.S.O. named Bullock came up with the Chongololo idea initially. He had great skills in producing a monthly magazine for children of studies in wildlife and the habitat, backed-up with a Teacher's Guide. This programme was to cover the whole of Zambia's Primary Schools. Mr Bullock was employed by the Society based in Lusaka whilst Jo made educational contributions and organised the regular distribution to schools of Copperbelt Province, coupled with wildlife film shows and expeditions organised by Noel Badrian, a young photographer by profession, whom she employed and paid from Branch funds. My two Game Rangers accompanied Noel giving him back-up with the local languages.

Chongololo, with the requisite fund raising to pay for our staff, grew to be a major business operation for Jo and I. We believed that wildlife education was the only long term means of preventing the total extermination of Africa's wildlife resource. This programme became genetically successful and can still be traced on-line, over forty years later. Jo's devotion to this cause was recognised by David Shepherd whom provided finance, long term.

Safer in the mountains?

Our son Richard's Save the Elephant poster

Rescued Genets lived in the house

Gray Mushau   Me   Adamson Lukuwu

CHAPTER ELEVEN

1977

Last year ended with the sale of 1000 Wildlife Society Calendars. This calendar illustrated **what to look out for** in the wild countryside month by month, with illustrations by our son Richard and some scenic photographs. This was to be a year of change for Jo and I, since my contract was due to terminate at the year-end, leaving us with the perilous option of joining the Zambian Government, or heading off for nowhere in particular. I was becoming well known in government circles, on account of my drafting the Third National Development Plan, TNDP, for the Copperbelt Province, and writing speeches for various District Governors – who were ignorant about rural affairs. All this was from the Cabinet Minister's Office in Ndola. Jo was dedicated to her wildlife conservation education programme with, as she declared, "A distant prospect of seeing my children again one day."

"Brian; I'm not sure where you're heading?" Jo enquired one day, looking searchingly into my eyes, "I am not over enamoured with the idea of becoming a Zambian, much as I am committed to the Wildlife Society."

"The Cabinet Minister has been pressing me very hard to consider a seat in the National Assembly with his guarantee of a ministerial post in rural development. Being a One Party State he can do that."

"Yes, well, do you think you could let little old me know; is it to be me and the kids, or, life as a white skinned Zambian? Answer by tea-time please."

"Oh."

Zambia was in dire economic trouble in 1977 because the copper price on the world market had plummeted. Adding to this Zambia's other export commodity; tobacco, was suffering from the European campaign to stop people smoking. However, I predicted this would be a temporary glitch; the Chinese are heavy smokers. Food shortages were pressing hard as well as every-day necessities disappearing through lack of foreign exchange for imports. Jo's sister was sending us toilet rolls and soap, with obvious implications. They were issuing import licences for cine projectors, alcohol, building materials, but not for hoes, bicycles, maize seed, tractor spares like tyres, animal feed supplements, corn milling plant spares, stock-feed vitamin supplements etc. Political speeches were always 'fighting talk' against Rhodesia and South Africa instead of resolving social problems 'at home'. *Hmm; sounds like 2018 UK!* Zambia

Government certainly needed a 'rural-people-minded' minister, regardless of skin colour, if they were going to develop a home grown food supply.

"Milk Brian?"

"Er, yes please. That'll be from Kafubu Dairy Farm. They'll manage without me."

"Is that it then? Always was a man of few words. I love you."

March 1977

President Kaunda was in Europe canvassing for money. He was an impressive personality and achieved some success; West Germany fell for KK's blarney and donated 25 million kwacha, £12,500,000, for Rhodesian refugees. Well, we did have Rhodesian African refugees in the Copperbelt Province; one was the Editor of the Mining Gazette, there were numerous business men, and there was a group of farmers in Ndola Rural District who, annoyingly, took all the prizes at the annual agricultural shows. KK did particularly well when he went to China. They were short of copper, and tobacco!

Zambia at this time was surrounded by nations in strife. There was talk of KK declaring war on Rhodesia but I felt confident that this was just a rallying call to impress friendly nations like Britain at the time of Iain Smith's Declaration of UDI, [United Declaration of Independence]. War had already broken out in neighbouring Congo. President Mobutu was making a plea to KK for help and to USA for a plane load of Coke Cola to be included in the Aid that USA was sending. The White House responded; "If President Mobutu wants Coke, he can buy it like everyone else." The Washington Post reported subsequently that Mobutu did in fact buy a load from USA for his troops. The Times of Zambia reported that his troops included Pygmy warriors who were spear-heading government troops in Shaba Province, specializing in the use of poison arrows. A local reporter said "....we are sure of destroying the enemy, whereas with bullets there are always survivors, and the Red Cross often intervenes. After poisoned arrows we send in commandoes. 150 – 200 Pygmies were involved in the fighting, and they make their arrow heads out of Coke Cola cans sent to us by USA. Pygmies are very dangerous warriors."

The Zambian Press reported; 'Real progress is being made in Zambia today. Here is the 1976 Annual Report by the Chairman of a well known Ndola company which is suffering from lack of import licences for their vital raw materials: "I am proud to say that absenteeism, pilfering and strikes have been considerably reduced during the year. I would like to pay tribute to all the people who serve this Corporation. Their hard work and loyalty have sustained the Corporation during these hard times. Even though for most of the year the workers did not have much work to do, they managed to report for work on time and sat around and chatted away for the boring and long hours. This shows the maturity of our workers and the dedication that they have to the Corporation. I am confident that we shall be reporting a further reduction in our losses in 1977." Signed, *Comrade Bonzo.*

Jo and I visited *Jimmy Rankin* at Miengwe Farm, bordering Miengwe Settlement Scheme, a Zambian white man born in Chief Nkambo's area. "I have learned seven Zambian tribal languages." he said "I have lived and worked amongst the Lamba people all my life, and I can say that I have no idea at all what might motivate or inspire any Lamba African to act upon his own initiative in joining your scheme Brian. The tribal African seems to have no constructive purpose in this world in his own right." Jimmy agreed with the policy of the Ministry of Rural Development in its effort to increase food production and cash cropping, but "It will take time, and there are no short cuts via education, 'freebies', or loans. Leaping forward is not on." We agreed that, the Department of Agriculture's political campaign to get villagers to grow one extra bag of maize per year was of dubious merit, and in reality commercial farming, employing the villagers, was the only way forward at a time of crisis. Thus, secure State Land tenure was now essential to attract private capital investment, as was planned for Mpongwe Development Zone.

Jimmy Rankin was an interesting character, emanating from Zambian soil. He was a pioneer, educated in USA under the auspices of the Seventh Day Adventist Church, but now living in a 'Kimberly mud brick' house with a thatched roof, financed by an Indian trader. His mother had a house with a corrugated iron roof and his father was buried under a tall *Albizia* tree near-by. Jimmy was tall, ginger haired with a bushy moustache, whilst his diminutive Japanese-looking wife apparently hated the Lamba as much as Jimmy loved them. Never the less they had produced two gorgeously beautiful girls that did not resemble their father at all but looked distinctly oriental with their jet black hair. I thought at the time that Jimmy should have been an anthropologist. I detected a desire for change and there was an expressed desire to set up a modern medical service centre of some kind, perhaps for dentistry.

Talking of anthropologists; one *Hortense Powdermaker* wrote a book entitled *Luanshya, Copper Mining Town.* She studied the African character and history up to Independence in 1964. Her book is a substantial tome. Here are some quotes from her book:
Population of whites on the Copperbelt 35,000, mainly British.
Population of Africans on the Copperbelt 250,000.
Population of Asians on the Copperbelt 600.

'The British mining community lived better than their counterparts in other parts of the world, with top class schools, clubs, recreational and medical facilities. History rather than biology determines the difference between the races. African societies are all egalitarian, but status is everything.'

'Fundamental to power in all regions of Africa is land and ancestral spirits. Supernatural power in the universe is still a common belief, it is called witchcraft. The first Europeans to come to Northern Rhodesia were missionaries. The missionaries all championed individualism rather than traditional collectivism. Zambians are not deeply religious like American Negroes, hence better integration with the modern world. Afrikaners suppressed Africans as inferior beings but the British taught the Africans trades and set up schools. N.R. became a Protectorate, rather than a Colony, in 1924. In 1953 the Federation took the land away from the Africans, hence the Africans hatred of Welensky. The British Government talked of Independence. Many white people who had settled in Northern Rhodesia permanently as miners, railway workers, and farmers &c and did not agree with Independence. It was said that European children growing up in N.Rhodesia felt superior to Africans. It was not until 1960 that a law was passed allowing Africans to enter shops and places of entertainment.'

My comment: There was no such racial discrimination when Jo and I arrived in Zambia in 1967. We would not have gone there had there been any hint of that. We knew nothing of the history delineated by Hortense Powdermaker, but the hatred for the Federation soon aroused our curiosity. The African community loved the 'movies' in the mine township, especially our wildlife films, which they could relate to. Their other favourites were definitely Cowboys and the Wild West. I frequently heard them appraise the fist fights, however on the subject of gun fights they often said "Guns are for shooting animals not people, America must be a very violent society." How true that has proved to be.

In January it had come to my ears that one J.M.Zulu, an early settler in Miengwe whom I knew very well, was having serious social problems despite his attempted leadership with community projects like self-help school building. He was not a Lamba but had worked in town and had learned to speak English very well, hence tended to speak up for the tribe in public affairs. His wife was an Ngoni. His leadership was resented even after many years; villagers gossiped that "He thinks he's a European. He has built a large fancy brick house and erects notices outside his farm." I was told that when he was away they let out his chickens and pull up his onions. His efforts are unwelcome he said to me, and he was thinking of leaving. He said, "I fear for my family. I paid heavily for my wife and promised to protect her. The risk has become too great. If my wife is poisoned I shall have a heavy fine to pay to her people." In April I checked up on his case and found that Mr Zulu was still settled.

April1977.
March-winds heralded marching caterpillars. They were almost totally be-whiskered, large, and marching like soldiers armoured with gold and green spikes all along their segments. They moved in lines, nose to tail, presumably to ensure that they all arrive together at where-ever they were going, and pupate together. They reminded us of the 22,000 Chinese 'engineers' building the railway, all alike in grey serge uniforms, thinking alike, all smoking, crowding the food stores in Ndola on occasion and buying up all the chocolates. The caterpillars were marching together from a favourite tree to another tree in the impending rainy season; the Chinese were marching together from Dar es Salaam to Kapiri Mposhi, over a thousand miles, and several rainy seasons.

Partly because of shortages a serious crime wave had developed in Ndola, both the criminals and the Police were armed. We all had security guards on our houses, to which our two geese added an alarm signal whenever a stranger appeared, that is until they disappeared into the township for someone's supper. Things were not going well for the nation; a gang of terrorists were challenging the political constitution. This gang lived upon the wild 'game' around the Copperbelt Province fringes. Jo and I were in Itimpi Forest Reserve checking up on my bulldozers, doing clearing work for Chris Davis, Plantations Manager, when we found ourselves confronted by the army. They told us that they had shot dead a band of Mashala guerrillas that morning. So even in my work place lawlessness had appeared.

On the eighteenth of April a near total eclipse of the sun occurred setting the nation into a state of alarm, being unpredicted. On the plus side however, superstitious minds resulted in the crime scene becoming noticeably subdued.

Jo wrote in the W.L.C.S.Z. Newsletter MFUBU:
'Brian rescued a baby Sykes Blue monkey to accompany our adult Sykes Blue mother we call Emily. We have named the little chap Henry. I take Henry under my shirt when I go out shopping in Ndola and he sometimes pops his head up to see what's going on and his bright eyes and whiskers between my breasts causes some alarm amongst both black and white shoppers in the food store. Emily is a clever monkey and resents strongly being shut in the garage when we are cleaning out. Last week she showed her resentment by unscrewing all the jars of screws and nails above

Brian's work bench and throwing the contents all over the floor. We watched her through the garage window assiduously working on the garage door lock with a piece of wire. The Sykes Blue is quite a rare monkey and makes a pet because it does not have those large canine biting teeth that the common grey Vervet does. Sykes feed on leaves in the canopy of evergreen trees. Brian found Emily with a wire tied tight round her waist cutting into the flesh whilst on sale in the market. She has become gentle and quite lovable but will have to be returned to the wild later this year.'

Jo's message continued:

'I have two rescued genets living loose in my house; they are tiny like weasels, untiringly energetic and playful. They were very easy to house-train to a litter box like a cat. They entertain my coffee morning ladies, climbing up the curtains and hiding in the pelmets, their big bright eyes and be-whiskered faces peeping out with a mischievous look and all the time chattering, echoing the gossip going on below.'

'My pet cheetah Che-Che is another absolute charmer, never aggressive, and more dog-like than cat-like. I sometimes think it is wrongly classified as cat family, not having retractable claws. It travels happily on the back seat of my car like any dog, terrifying any potential thieves more than the Police presence in the market. No doubt she can move faster than my old Peugeot on grassy plains, and on solar energy too. However she doesn't need to out-run me in the dambo because she gets waste meat from a farmer friend and has no need to exert her-self. She is on loan from the Munda Wanga Zoo in Lusaka hence will be returned there when we leave at the end of the year.'

'Our wildlife safari school teacher Noel Badrian, has a pet Serval Cat that accompanies him on his school rounds to the children's delight and is charming and playful. I will see if I can get a photo for the newsletter. Its long legs are not for running, like the Cheetah, but for leaping. It can spring high in the air and drop on its prey like an eagle. It does not spot its prey like a raptor from above but by acute hearing with its large ears. This very beautiful spotted cat has, sadly, become very rare in the wild and is on the Endangered Species list.'

The Society members had raised funds to finance the employment of Noel Badrian full time, distributing the Chongololo Magazine and Teachers Guide to all Primary Schools in the Province, with emphasis upon the rural areas. Our two game rangers accompanied him with the film projector unit when they were not on road block and patrol duties.

Jo was still running her private school for tutoring expatriate children who were faced with overseas boarding school exams. She used the PNEU

Course which is designed for Embassy Overseas Service and other such personnel. She is a natural born teacher, very strict, which is why the children love her, it's all about justice and trust. Her mother was a nanny to the aristocracy, in particular to Peter Scott when his father was in the Antarctic and then to Lord Killearn before WWI. Hence her knowledge of training children was conveyed to Jo during WWII. We subsequently hosted Sir Peter Scott in his Copperbelt fund raising visit. Jo was totally committed to the Chongololo wildlife education campaign since we believed this was the only long term hope for conservation of wildlife in Africa. This programme is still running in Zambia, serving all junior schools in the nation in 2017, with support from the David Shepherd Wildlife Foundation. On the other side of our conservation campaign we were having a tough time against poachers.

At Masaiti Agricultural Show
Jo changed her image for the day

Land clearing for Forestry Plantations

Termite mound

Grey Mushitu   Adamson Lukuwo

Brian's Badge

Che-Che in her pen

Our Genets

Jo's Genet

Noel Badrian's
Serval Cat

Our Caracal

Golden Tamarin from S.America at our Zoo.

A guest

Emily

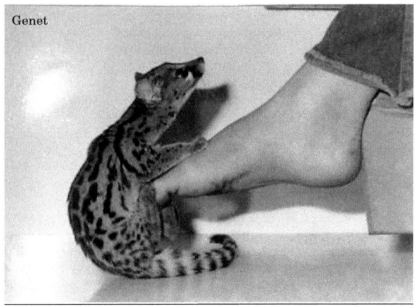

Genet

219

Here is an example:

<u>WLCSZ anti-poacher Report</u>
'During the dry season our activities are mainly week-end operations in the bush, which are inaccessible during the rains. On our last big operation was an area close to Kafue National Park. We were combined with the Copperbelt Unit, and the outcome of the operation was 71 arrests, one poacher shot and killed, one wounded, and the confiscation of eleven vehicles, 18 firearms, 2,400 rounds of ammunition and 3-4 tons of game meat. This was over a period of 44 hours of ploughing through rough bush, raiding poacher's camps, guarding prisoners during the night (we ran out of handcuffs), fighting off what seemed to be the entire tsetse fly population of Zambia, repairing faulty vehicles and so forth. It is small wonder that we arrived back home ready for 12 hours sleep and not looking forward to 'the office' next day. The cost of petrol for this type of operation is financed by the WLCSZ and can amount to several hundred kwachas for a week-end.' *Jan Church, Senior Wildlife Ranger.*

'An exercise of this sort is directed mainly against commercial poaching, which is creating the greatest threat to wildlife existence. The villager who snares a duiker for the pot is no danger, he has been doing it for centuries and his activities have had a negligible effect – and often it his only source of protein. The danger is the semi-permanent poaching camps, set up in remote areas, sometimes one, sometimes several, scattered over an area. From these camps hunters go out on foot and shoot game, usually at night. When an animal is killed, its whereabouts is reported to the camp and carriers go out and bring the animal back, sometimes whole, sometimes butchered where it falls. The meat is then smoked on racks over fires, then packed into sacks and taken to the Copperbelt where it is sold illegally, often in bars. It is a highly organised operation and when the game in an area has been wiped out, the poachers move to another area and so it goes on. They kill anything that moves and the men in the camps live rough and get paid little.'

Jo and I went down to Lusaka for a Wildlife Society Council meeting by plane because we were to collect our new VW Kombi bus for transporting up to 30 school children to the Educational Centre on Busanga Plains in the north region of Kafue National Park. We met up again with Jan Church and also Norman Carr of Luangwa Valley who was planning a unique Walking Safari challenge for tourists. We agreed to join him in July. Norman was already internationally famous because of his books and a film about his two tame lions.

Whilst in Lusaka we took advantage of my boss's invitation to spend a week-end down south sailing on Kafue Dam reservoir. His wife Sheila came and an old friend from ODA in London training days, Jim Mansfield with whom I had the same interests and skills. As to dinghy sailing skills Jo and I thought that would be a walk-over with our Indian Ocean sailing club expertise, however we came in, shamefully, second, hence delegated to doing the braai – the Afrikaans word for barbecued meat with spices.

There was a three day public holiday in May. Jo and I took off for Mpongwe, where we had our Sprite caravan at the time, about fifty miles south of Ndola. I had a new scheme nearby called Mikata one acre tobacco scheme, fashioned upon my Oxfam Matwiga tobacco scheme in Tanzania, with a borehole for water in that very remote woodland; my road grader following a route cleared by some sturdy axmen, and there was help with free USA World Food Programme food, which all such programmes need in the first year of settlement in a new area. Working in the Cabinet Office gave me access to such services without argument. The soil was very sandy and excellent for quality Virginia tobacco, as per Rhodesia. This was village level development, not capital intensive modern mechanised farming, and utilising some of the hundreds of 45 gallon oil drums left over from oil imports, as tobacco curing ovens. The settlers were a cheery crowd, singing songs to greet us when they heard the name Dawtrey. Jo got the gathering of women laughing before we left, so we were all happy.

After a swim in Inampamba Lake we headed for the Mpongwe Swedish Mission Hospital. They had built a water tower with a guest apartment at the top with fabulous views of the countryside. The long winding wooden staircase set off my lumbago necessitating my sojourn on the hard floor instead of the comfy bed with Jo. The next day we could see the vast Mwinuna Plains southwards towards Lukanga Swamps in Central Province to which we wanted to find the motor track which the fishermen used to bring their fish to the Copperbelt. Elizabeth Smith my young Assistant, geography graduate had volunteered to undertake the arduous exercise of surveying the new State Land boundary about 45 miles south of Mpongwe near Lukanga Swamps, living under canvass with Zambian assistant surveyors for weeks at a time. She had the true pioneering spirit.

We had good news from a local Ndola printing company director. He succumbed to Jo's sense of humour and agreed to print one thousand 1978 Wildlife Society Calendars free of charge. The draft contained many of Richard's drawings of plants, animals, birds and butterflies. His art work is rooted in his successful 'nature studies' at Arusha School in Tanzania and his life as a boy on the farm in England. I do the 'what to look for' month by month in the Calendar.

Our new Provincial Agricultural Officer called me. Here was a very different person to J.E. Chikoti, smart suit, commanding presence despite his small stature, and speaking beautiful English with great depth of vocabulary which enabled him to 'hold the floor' with ease. I thought he was a man of some administrative and perhaps political potential. As ever the thought in my mind was *could he achieve anything in the field?* He told me that the Prime Minister was coming to tour Mpongwe Development Zone.

"I don't know anything about your projects down there Mr Dawtrey, can you please conduct the Prime Minister and his team in my place. He'll be here at 6.0 am on Saturday."

So, all day Saturday and Sunday I was out with Elijah Mudenda the PM, plus his entourage; the Cabinet Minister for Copperbelt, Members of UNIP Central Committee, the District Governor, the Permanent Secretary for Agriculture, the Kabwe District Manager of the Tobacco Board of Zambia, the Press and TV.

The Tobacco Board of Zambia is an organisation that produces tobacco commercially as in Rhodesia, and trains Africans to use modern techniques and eventually to qualify for loans from whence they become tenants of the Board. The Board is starting such a scheme in the new Zone in the south of Mwinuna, to be accessed by a good gravel road to be built shortly. Looking at these two schemes for Virginia tobacco production, an important export crop was the purpose of the visit. We were an entourage of some dimension! Fifteen Land Rovers, about fifty officials, driving, driving, driving, through clapping and singing crowds where there was a village, with stops for the Prime Minister to proclaim with platitudinous speeches, credit for the immense development that the United National Development Party was achieving in this area. Actually there was only one person whom actually knew what was going on in this rural area – me. There was a group of my supporters, however, philosophically enjoying the shade of the veranda at Mpongwe Mission Hospital. These were local chiefs and district councillors.

Quietness prevailed eventually as we endured the pot-holes and muddy lake-like stretches where the road used to be. Mwinuna was a wild unpopulated vastness, 100 miles out of Copperbelt civilisation. Mpongwe Development Zone was about 10,000 square miles. We did eventually reach the new tenant tobacco scheme with its training institution and its keen young educated men and wives, a genuinely pioneering group.

On the way back we visited Kashiba Lake, now declared a National Monument under the overall plan for Mpongwe Development Zone, and then to the Mpongwe Farmer Training Centre for refreshment. How our old friend Reverend Peter Bugg, an agricultural missionary who set-up the training centre a few years ago, would have loved to have been there for this occasion. It became dark, 8.30 pm. The day had been intensely political with technical knowledge zero except for me; "Oh Mr Dawtrey, can we have your professional advice upon how and where we should create an access road to the tobacco scheme."

I attended a good-bye ceremony at 7.0 am on the Monday morning at Ndola Airport. The National Press was already full of pictures of maize and wheat trials with politicians, fields of tobacco plants with politicians, crowds of waving children with politicians, farmers at the Farmer Training Centre drinking tea with politicians. No mention of the proposed access road to Mwinuna or the actual location of these developments. I got the impression that the pressmen did not really know what the event was all about.

The following article was published by the London Times Supplement in March 1977:
'Zambia has one of the largest areas of fertile land that is not in production in Africa and the Colonial Development Corporation has been buying up state farms and investing millions of dollars to make them viable. The CDC is a majority stakeholder in Mpongwe Development Company, a farm in one of the most fertile areas and one of the biggest agricultural enterprises in the country. Mr Mtambo says "CDC farms are the biggest single producers of maize, wheat and soya beans in the country, and also produces 75% of the coffee.. CDC is spending $26 million on expanding Mpongwe and a further £8 million on Munkumpu Research Station acquired by CDC for $7.2 million." Mr Mtambo also says. "It makes sense to have a mill for downstream processing, and so a $10 million mill has been built at Kitwe in the Copperbelt, which now outputs between five and seven tonnes of maize and wheat a day." My air photo of the Mpongwe Farm was taken in 1987, courtesy of Landell Mills.

"In fact it is the single biggest producer in the country of maize, and it produces 75 per cent of the coffee. It is also the single biggest producer of wheat and soya beans," says Mr Mtamboh.

CDC is spending $26 million on expanding Mpongwe and a further $8 million on Mukumpu, another farm acquired by CDC for $7.2 million. Mr Mtamboh says that, as CDC's farms are the biggest producers of maize and wheat, it would make sense to have a mill for downstream processing. So a $10 million mill was built at Kitwe in the Copperbelt, and this now outputs between five and seven tonnes of wheat and maize a day.

Turkish tobacco - Mwinuna.

Cavendish banana trial,
Munkumpu.

*Mpongwe CDC wheat
and soya bean farm.*

Aerphoto courtesy Landell Mills 1987

Boreholes in the Mpongwe limestone   *Soil research Dr Peter Heilman*

7-7-77 my lucky number from WWII survival in the Coventry Blitz

Jo and I took off on this date in a Hawker Siddley748 at 11.0 am, landing at noon in Luangwa Valley National Park for the event of a lifetime, walking with Norman Carr for seventy five miles in untamed 'bush' country as Africa was in the Victorian era. It turned out to be no more dangerous than Central London. Night stops were temporary straw built camps prepared ahead of us, with food and drinks. We were a small group with an armed Game Guard ahead of us and a 'Tea-boy' behind with a tea pot on his head for mid-day revival.

Upon our first arrival in the Valley a Game Ranger picked us up at the airstrip in a VW converted Kombi and drove us, with four other guests, the forty miles to Chipembe Lodge. The *Mopani* woodland seemed endless, but still green despite the height of the dry season. No wonder the elephants love this area. We received a warm welcome at the Lodge, sited on the Luangwa River bank, from people we knew from the Game Department and of course Norman Carr. There was good news about NSEFU. This was a chiefs area outside the park where a trial to give the hunting control of licensing to the Chief and his people instead of central government, and it was proving successful in eliminating poaching. They had learned that the wildlife was their natural resource and no questions were being asked as to how they protected it, as they enjoyed the benefit derived from the substantial income from licences. Hence 'game' were on the increase.

We relaxed under the deep shade of *Trichilia emetica* trees along the river bank with our Pimms, watching the hugely fat hippos grunting with satisfaction in the warm murky river. We were not supposed to be luxuriating in the Lodge, this was a Walking Safari, and hence we were accommodated that night in a nearby grass hut. We rose at dawn, 6.0 am, and set off on foot, wading a cool river in the chill morning air and rolling mist, hoping there weren't any male hippos suffering from a bad night's grazing. We walked twelve miles and found a grass hutted camp called Mwemba, which bore the designation Executive Camp. This was to become a camp for distinguished visitors. I gathered that at a later date these included David Shepherd, Sir Peter Scott, and Prince Bernhardt of the Netherlands. This was a delightful spot situated on a lagoon where elephants drifted down to in the moonlight. The elephants were not afraid of our torches flashing on them, almost as though they didn't see them.

The next camp was difficult to reach. This was a clay area and the elephants had heavily trodden it in the rainy season hence now baked hard was an ankle breaker to walk over. Norman Carr was now with us for the rest of the way, so we sat chatting round the camp fire in the long dark evenings, mostly about elephants and their twenty million years of domination in Africa, and their unpredictable behaviour. Norman expressed disgust at the plan, by the UN Food and Agriculture Organisation to build a meat factory in the southern area of the park, to 'crop' the elephants that are said to be "overgrazing the Mopani woodlands". The plan is to supply meat to the Copperbelt Province he said. "The UN suffers from over academy in their staff selection in my experience." Norman will collect statistics of the decline in elephant numbers for my record [Herewith; see Appendix].

Norman told us about the recent memorial stone placed in the park by Philip Berry the current Warden and Safari Guide for tourists. It was dated 8th August 1973 and marked the spot in the park where a well know Game Warden; Johnny Van Uys, was killed by an elephant. Norman had a lot of valuable statistics about wildlife in the natural world which I noted in my diary. To cut a long story short we trekked bravely for days and days, amongst herds of Cape Buffalo numbered in hundreds, lions disturbed from dozing in long grass fled in all directions, and amazingly wading across the rivers amongst crocodiles that did not arouse a moments' concern. It appears that Luangwa crocs are a subspecies of the killers in the Kafue River, and any way they have got plenty to eat without risking human flesh, not forgetting that we did have an armed Game Guard.

227

Luangwa River.

Posh bedrooms in the bush.

Hippos kill more people than crocodiles.

Norman Carr

Walking safari date 7.7.77

Tea Boy.

Five days walk - 75 miles

The secretive Kudu

September 1977

We are winding up our personal affairs. Jo placed a plea in our Newsletter: '**Sophie** is a baboon that lives in our Trade Fair Zoo grounds. She has lived with us since 1971, one of many rescued animals. She has given pleasure to those of us looking after her and to the hundreds who visited our Zoo during the Trade Fair week, which was not always fun for Sophie because she was often given offensive things like lighted cigarettes.

Our two Sykes Blue Monkeys, Emily and Henry will be returned to the wild near the Kafue River and Machiya. Brian and I are leaving Zambia soon but we cannot return Sophie to the wild because baboons are very gregarious and if she tried to join another troop they would kill her as an 'illegal immigrant'. Mrs O'Dell the farmer has been helping to feed her along with Mrs Scott and Mrs Price, feeding her one day a week. During my stay in Africa over the last sixteen years I have been given many wild animals and I have not lost faith in human nature. There must be someone who will undertake to adopt Sophie as a pet at home to avoid having to 'put her down'. My phone number is Ndola 82520. Many thanks to all those members who have been such a help in the past.' *End of Appeal*

October 1977

Having relinquished my chairmanship of the Copperbelt Branch of W.L.C.S.Z I was presented, ceremoniously, with a hefty book entitled *The Atlas of World Wildlife* signed by scores of treasured names of key members of the Society from all over Zambia. Che-Che had been returned to the Munda Wanga Game Department Zoo in Lusaka, along with the Caracal, the Genets and some others, leaving us with our two Sykes Blue tree canopy monkeys. We loaded the pair into the car closeted in a small cage that they were familiar with and set off one rainy day, to find a patch of *mushitu* evergreen woodland we knew of down near Machiya and the Kafue River. *Mushitu* is an African word for an unusual type of forest populated by tall evergreen species mainly *Syzygium vitalis* which thrive in a wetland habitat and are associated with *Ficus spp.* of fruiting edible fig trees which also depend upon a high water table. It was a long drive, about 100 miles.

We sat down in our selected spot for a picnic with the cage alongside. Jo opened the door and their heads popped out quizzically. "Off you go Emily and Henry." Jo said sadly "Plenty of food here, and no nasty trappers." It started spitting with rain so we put up my big survey umbrella while Jo lit our Primus for tea. Quite cosy really, sitting in our camp chairs to a chorus of bird song. Low and behold we were joined by two monkeys sheltering from the rain.

Our House Contents Sale at No 8 Buseko Avenue, Itawa, was somewhat heart breaking in many ways but there was one item which was a triumph of goodwill, for the credit of the Society funds. We sold our David Shepherd print of a bull elephant with Mt Kilimanjaro in the background for £680, K 1360. When David was staying with us he remarked that this was his first elephant painting and now quite rare. I actually purchased it in Dar es Salaam in 1962 for thirty shillings from an Indian duka in the days when we didn't know who DS.was but thought *by Jove that's a good painting must have that for our house;* in the mountains of Mbeya. The proceeds from our sale of chattels were substantial, however the money deposited in the Bank was to be held there until foreign exchange became available, which meant that we could not externalize the proceeds to help us set up a home in England. There was a queue, the bank manager said, of indeterminant length.

KK confidentially said "The veil of civilization is thin and needs two generations of escape from oppressive tribalism and superstition to lift the veil. For the black man the past always beckons." I shall for ever remember Daniel Chintilye with a tear in my eye as a great educated leader in this Ndola Rural community. His Reference below:

NDOLA RURAL COUNCIL

Telephone 2806 - 22

P.O. Box 397

Luanshya

Zambia

IN REPLY PLEASE QUOTE
REF. No. NRC/AD/72. VOL. III - 673

Date 4th October 19 77

TO WHOM IT MAY CONCERN

MR. B. DAWTREY

While we are still on earth, we make friends of people we have loved for their good relationships in the way they have shared problems with us.

Soon or later time to depart comes. In most cases departure is influenced by circumstances beyond our control.

On behalf of the Ndola Rural Council and indeed on my own behalf, time has come to say goodbye to the Dawtrey family who are leaving this Province and District. There is not much that can be said of him other than saying how much this Council has been impressed by his work as Provincial Planning Officer during these difficult years.

His plans to develop this area have been wonderful and progressive. During the 2nd National Development Plan. His work can clearly be seen by having established settlement sechemes such as Miengwe Village Regrouping, Mikata Family Farms and the Munkumpu proposed wheat schemes in Chief Ndubeni's Area to mention only few and etc.

The District has been enlightened for many more successes in future in as far as Rural Development is concerned. Surely without his dedication and the spirit of sacrifice and service to the people, he would have not accomplished what now has remained history and credit to his name for-ever.

We wish Mr. Dawtrey and family a happy stay wherever he is going and he should also carry with him the happy memories of places and friends he has created down here. Our Council will remain open to receive him back some day should the trend of things make it that way. God be with you.

D.S. CHINTILYE
CHAIRMAN
NDOLA RURAL COUNCIL

DSC/NN.

c.c. The Permanent Secretary, Copperbelt Province,
P.O. Box 153, NDOLA.

c.c. The Provincial Agric. Officer, P.O. Box 232, NDOLA.

c.c. The District Secretary, Ndola Rural District,
P.O. Box 50, MASAITI.

We took the Hawker Sidley 748 to Lusaka and picked up the VC 10 for Gatwick, our boxes of treasured personal effects would follow in due course and go into a storage godown at Garwick Airport awaiting Customs Clearance and further instructions.

"Toodle-Pip Zambia."

CHAPTER TWELVE

1977

Beyond every romantic story there is reality
We arrived at Gatwick well before dawn on 30th October. Jo persuaded one of the airline staff to run us into Crawley in an official car, to our old Tanzanian friends Jean and Eric Wrintmore's house. We dragged them out of bed for some breakfast and enjoyed a riotous welcome from everyone, their children also, now suddenly it seemed, adults. Their son David was working as a green keeper at the Golf Club, the 'nearest he could get to the wilds of Tanzania' he said. Jane announced her engagement to a long haired youth in a scary leather motor cycle rider's outfit; "We are both animal lovers" she announced "We are going to have a small farm for breeding goats, and guinea pigs."

Eric was an Appeal Court Judge in London. He took us on the commuter train to his Chambers from which we made our way to the government offices of the Overseas Development Administration – ODA. The Staff were totally ignorant of what we had been doing for the last sixteen years, despite them having recruited me and paid my salary supplement, gratuity, and air fares for us and our children. They searched through their files again;

"Ah, here we are, Brian Dawtrey Field Officer/Agriculture, Tanganyika."

"Actually; Provincial Planning Officer, Copperbelt Province, Zambia." I retorted.

After a long search; "I see we have a vacancy in Papua New Guinea for an Agricultural Adviser."

"That's not my discipline; try Land-use Planning."

"Oh. What about this; Solomon Islands – Fisheries Officer?"

Next stop World Bank Office. We met the bright and welcoming Secretary.

"Ah, I have a message for you Brian. Please call Paddy Fleming. He is in Norfolk at the moment. I'll call him up, do take a seat. Coffee? "

In the outcome I spoke to Paddy, whom I had met once in Lusaka, Zambia. He said he knew all about my work in land development and that I was just what he needed for his new World Bank Integrated Rural Development Project in Ayangba, Southern Nigeria. I told him that I had written to Washington DC already, looking for a vacancy and they had replied that I did not have the necessary academic qualifications for consideration for a post with the Bank. Paddy responded; "Oh take no notice of them, I'm managing this project for the Bank, and I need people who can do the job. You will be contracted to the Bank of course, top flight tax-free salary paid in US dollars. You would be designated Chief Land-Use Planning Officer, officially, but there will be a lot more to it than that I think. You'll need to get your wife to agree because the climate is hell and you'll have to build yourself a house, in the rain forest. Igalaland is a primitive place which is why we a going there, you'll have to let me know whether you can both face it. We have thirty million dollars to spend, starting in March."

Subject to reading Paddy's background manuscript we felt elated, and back in Crawley we were chirpy enough to go down the road and buy a Peugot 104 car, for cash! Yes we could do that with our gratuity, we felt like the idle rich for a few weeks. We finally found our youngest son Philip living on the edge of the New Forest near Southampton. He introduced us to an extrovert young lady named Barbara and announced his engagement. We were delighted with the prospect of increasing our family yet again. The die was cast; we needed to look for a house in the New Forest; the nearest habitat we might find to Africa.

We found an ex-vicarage for £34,000 and a bungalow amongst the ponies for £23,000. Jo immediately fell in love with the latter of course, and we instructed the Agent in Lymington to purchase for £22,000 after they advised us that it had been on the market for a year and that no-one was buying property in Britain these days. We offered cash-down from our U.S savings that we had made by transferring out of sterling during the 'crash'. It would in the outcome, take three months for the slumbering Lymington Solicitor to get the keys.

"What now Brian, is our future to be in the New Forest or the tropical rain forests of southern Nigeria, what did Fleming call the place?"

"Igalaland."

We set our compass to North and set off for Leamington Spa to see my sister Joy, her husband George, my mother, and inevitably the dreary line up of celebrities on TV. From thence we set off in our new Peugot 104 to challenge the glories of the M1 to West Yorkshire, where son Richard now lived with his Luanshya Mine Captain's daughter Ann. There was an expectant face in the window in hilly Highburton. It was a triumphant re-union, at long last, we loved it, and we stayed and stayed and stayed. With a Yorkshire grandchild looming we had a serious decision to finally make. We had until March anyway to get a roof over our heads in UK so off we went to San Francisco where our daughter Caroline now lived with Iain her shipping agent husband. We all drove to Vancouver for Christmas. We were forty nine years old and this was a very happy Christmas; with a totally blind view of our destiny.

I had received Paddy Fleming's memorandum and read it out to eager listeners:

'The fact that the salary is tax-free makes an astonishing difference to its value BUT there is a reason why it is high. There are no shops in Igalaland or indeed in Benue State at all. With a Land Rover one can reach Anambra State on the south coast with a stay-over in a hotel where there are good shops. Ayangba does have a busy street market every day, and a post office of sorts, but no telephones. The nearest Telex machine is in Kaduna 250 miles away. We will send a driver there once a week to make contact with the outside world. . The forest streams provide good clean water which can be collected by tanker. We will generate our own electricity. Humidity is 100% with the temperature reaching 45 degrees centigrade. The sky is a haze over the forest, like the Amazon. The Igala people are very friendly and they maintain their tribal culture and traditions with pride under their King. The area is isolated geographically by the confluence of two mighty rivers, the Niger and the Benue. The Benue State Capital town is Makurdi, where there is a bridge to the north over the River Benue. This is reached by 40 miles of tar strip road from Ayangba. The native oil palm of the forest provides a valuable traditional rural industry. There are no hospital facilities or clinics but the Catholic Mission has a qualified lady doctor in Ayangba and there is a doctor at Idah Catholic Mission near the King's Palace on the river Niger. The Project area is about the size of Norfolk and the nearest airport is Kano on the Sahara Desert fringe about one thousand kilometres away, which is where you would arrive. I hope we (possibly you) can build an airstrip in Ayangba. We will build a club house with sports facilities and good staff houses. Do join us.'

This is Alhaji Aliyu Obaji CBE., CON. The Attah.

APPENDIX

List of birds seen in Luangwa Valley 7th July 1977

Wood Hoopoe, White Shouldered Blackbird, Black Heron, Nob Nose Duck, Squacco Heron, Pied Crow, Ground Hornbill, Spur wing Goose, Wattled Plover, White Headed Vulture, Glossy Starling, Roller, Grey Hornbill, Golden Oriole, Drongo, Creeping Francolin, Hammer Kop, Swallow – black and white, Namaqua Dove, Bee-eater - with green back, yellow bib and collar, Buzzard – with yellow eye, grey body, orange legs and bill, Helmeted Guinea Fowl, Walhberg's Eagle, Robin Chat, Ashy Flycatcher, Great White Heron, Small White Heron, Yellow Bulbul, Red Billed Waxbill, Brown Headed Kingfisher, Hornbill, Cisticolor, Grey Lowrie, Rock Dove, Red Eyed Dove, Scarlet-chested Sunbird, Egret, Red Necked Francolin, Shrike, Sparrow, Bateleur Eagle, Darter, Pied Kingfisher, Bishop Bird, Malachite Kingfisher.

Elephants – Loxodonta Africana

Length of tusks: male up to 20 feet; female up to 16 feet. Height of female: up to 8ft 6 inches; baby 2ft 9 inches at birth. Life span; about 60 years

Some population statistics: 2017

1. Luangwa Valley National Park, Zambia – total hunting ban.
   1973 100,000. 1988 25,000. *Zambia national total*   21,758 *stable*
2. Selous National Park, Tanzania – total hunting ban.
   1977 120,000. 1988 50,000. *Tanzania national total*   42,871 *declining*
3. Tsavo National Park, Kenya – total hunting ban.
   1968 40,000. 1988 5,700. *Kenya national total*   25,959 *stable*
4. Central African Republic – total hunting ban.
   1977 80 – 100,000. 1988 10 – 15,000.   *No figures*
5. Zimbabwe, whole nation – controlled hunting.
   1979 30,000. 1989 43,000. *Zimbabwe national total*   82,304 *declining*
6. Republic of South Africa National Parks – controlled culling.
   1979 7,000. 1989 8,200. *R.S.A. national total*   17,438 *increasing*
7. Botswana, whole nation – controlled hunting.
   1979 20,000. 1989 51,000. *Botswana national total*   130,451 *stable*

[Source; early stats. Iain Douglas Hamilton. Regional Game Departments.]

Commentary on elephants:

So why does 'controlled hunting' result in an increase in elephant numbers?

Game Management Areas operate licensed hunting to the benefit of the native population; hence the local people and their own selected Game Guards have a vested interest in driving out poachers, who tend to have mass slaughter tactics these days. Hence they are much more effective than 'centralised' government Game Guards working far from Base. Where licensed hunting is organised the proceeds go to pay salaries and services for the local area viz., in the case of GMA 23 Machiya, a school and a road.

Late news 2017; As a result of the Duke of Cambridge's visit in 2017, China has enacted a total ban on all trading in ivory.

Elephants are passive communicators, never silent.

Do elephants have long memories?

A factual case from South African records: ADDO NAT. PARK history; in 1910 when it was a farming area, an attempt was made to exterminate the whole herd of 140 elephants at the request of the farming community and in the interests of food production. A well known hunter named Pretorious killed them expertly, one by one. The event became deeply imprinted in the memory of the survivors. After a year of killing only 16 – 30 elephants remained and they were so wary that they never emerged from the forest in daylight. In 1930 Pretorious admitted defeat and Addo elephants were granted 8,000 acres of fenced sanctuary on a hillside. Today they have not changed their behaviour, even though they are never shot at, and they are said to be very dangerous. They are still nocturnal, even though there are no animals left alive from the 1910 - 1930 era. *It seems possible that this may be a DNA change?*

Lightning Source UK Ltd.
Milton Keynes UK
UKHW021022190719
346401UK00007B/66/P